LAMENTING THE LOSS OF LOYALTY

Where Has All The Loyalty Gone?!

LAMENTING THE LOSS OF LOYALTY

Where Has All The Loyalty Gone?!

K.L. Fischer PhD

K.L. Fischer Publications

Publisher: K.L. Fischer Publications

ISBN-13: 978-1978388673
ISBN-10: 1978388675

Table of Contents

To My Dear Reader

For me LOYALTY is the noblest of all human virtues. Therefore if we have lost it – either in our primary relationship – or outside our primary relationship – I promise to help us find it – and reclaim it – by giving us insights and support – to practice and experience it.

Hence this book is for me and mine and you and yours.

Where has all the loyalty gone? Long time passing. I for one lament its loss. And having brought up the subject with others have discovered I have plenty of company.

Most of us have more questions than answers about loyalty's demise:

- Gone? Gone for good?
- Will it ever come back?
- What happened that it's gone?
- Who cares that it's gone?
- Who needs it anyway?
- We don't need it – Do we?
- We can live without it – Can't we?
- What did we have to do with its leaving?
- What did others have to do with its leaving?
- If we think it's not important – How come it's not?
- If we care a great deal – Well, what then?

- If we couldn't care less – Well, how come?
- Do we even know what it looks like?
- Have we seen it in others?
- Have we seen it in ourselves?
- Summarily – Have we given up on it?
- Don't expect it – Don't look for it – Don't give it – Don't receive it?

Flash! Maybe we've been looking for it in all the wrong places!

So, therefore, let us contemplate – Reflect upon – Roll back our memories to when it was there in our lives – (If indeed, it ever was).

Let us see if we can't recover, restore, replenish this noblest of all human virtues that is the rubric LOYALTY – For the good of ourselves and others and the rest of mankind. Tall order, indeed – But worthy of our pervasive, persistent pursuit – Wouldn't we agree?

Contemplating the worthwhileness of our pursuit in the context of our lamenting loyalty's demise we reflect upon how realistic and feasible is our goal of reintroducing and refurbishing loyalty in our everyday lives.

Where do we start? How do we begin our quest for loyalty?

We begin with understanding more fully what we are looking for.

What does it mean to be a loyal person?

Let us keep in mind that it is not a given that we have experienced loyalty in our lifetime – A bold statement even as it is true.

Loyalty is not part of our genetic makeup. It is a construct of acquired qualities that a person may or may not develop (more or less of) through person perception and self experience.

A construct – a compilation – a clustering of qualities that come together under the rubric of loyalty.

To be a loyal person then means that we have more or less of these qualities in our personality.

Our human-ness and upbringing – Our unique one-of-a-kind personality development and self experience shape and mold us into the kind of person we end up being with respect to the qualities that make up loyalty.

But before we begin our quest for the meaning and efficacy of loyalty – in our lives and others – we need to ask ourselves once more whether our quest for loyalty will be worth it.

These days is being loyal a case of flying in the face of reality?

Has loyalty become archaic, an anachronism for our time, a forgotten, no longer relevant virtue?

Has it been replaced by something else – something less?

Do we need to change with the times with respect to the practice of loyalty?

Shall we concede that loyalty in today's world only makes sense in the context of our primary relationship (if we have one)? – That we should stop looking for it or practicing it outside our primary relationship?

So then, is one's primary relationship the last bastion of loyalty?!

Have we come full circle so that we have ended where we have started?! – Therefore, expect no loyalty beyond our primary relationship and we won't be disappointed.

Practice no loyalty beyond our primary relationship and we won't end up feeling used – Is this being cynical or realistic?! – Or is this being cynically realistic?!

If we find no loyalty out there – Shall we give up on being loyal out there?! – Or shall we continue to be loyal (if we are) and take our lumps?! – If we continue to do so – Are we just being naïve, foolish, a dreamer?!

If we have the characteristic of loyalty in our personality – How important is it to our self-concept, our self-worth?! – This is what we want to discern before we give up on loyalty outside our relationship with our primary other – Ask ourselves – Do we want to change this part of our personality because we don't perceive it in others besides ourselves?! – Keep in mind, however, that if this personality need to be loyal so dominates our personality that others perceive it in our presentation – "a mile away" – This is not a good thing for us. Metaphorically, "The tail is wagging the dog."

Our need in this case to be a loyal person – and to be in a relationship with a loyal person – conceivably may lead us to wishfully project onto the other qualities of loyalty – That just aren't there – Hence we end up seeing what we want to – and need to see – But were we to validate our expectations and assumptions – we'd come to realize that our need(s) clouded the reality of what we perceived – What we thought was there – to our dismay – Wasn't there – Let's not be unduly hard on ourselves in this case. This is the nature of perceptual judgments based primarily on what we need to perceive.

Still others may view the one – who presents their need to be loyal (with all its qualities) as "Ripe for the picking" – Us asking to be taken advantage of. Viewing the presenter's need to be loyal as an open invitation to be manipulated and subsequently abused by the other – The caveat when such occurs is not to allow such experiences to discourage us from continuing to value those qualities of loyalty we have introspectively and extrospectively discovered in ourselves and present them assertively and confidently for others to perceive.

However, the other caveat would be not to allow such experiences to discourage us from becoming more aware of – (having lowered our defense of projection) – the realities of what the other is in a position to – and willing to – offer us in return for our loyalty – Before we expect any semblance of reciprocity.

Therefore, let us not allow these caveats to change our desire to perceive ourselves – and have others perceive us – as a loyal person. Keep in mind we can only control what we present. What the other perceives – and what they do with it – is not within our purview of control.

We present qualities of loyalty because they (these) we have come to understand are part of who we are – In doing so we may be making ourselves vulnerable to those who perceive our presentation in this way – Vulnerable in what way(s)? – That depends upon what the perceiver brings to the interaction – Keep in mind – Early on we really don't know what the perceiver is thinking or feeling about what we're presenting – Our qualities of loyalty may be looked upon by some as weakness or naïveté – Or as premature – not fitting the other's perception of what should be transpiring – Too much, too soon – Not to be matched by where the other "is at."

Others – upon our presentation of qualities of loyalty – may introspectively respond within – to look for such qualities within themselves – and coming up short – may decide not to engage any further – Or at least to lessen their participation in interacting – Realizing they can't come close to what we are presenting – and (in their mind) are "asking for."

I'm guessing that by now we are anxious to know what qualities of loyalty we've been talking about in our quest for them – Incidentally, but importantly – these qualities which make up the rubric loyalty – That we look for within ourselves – and consider presenting to others – outside our primary relationship – are the same qualities we eventually will bring into our primary relationship. These are the following.

Trustworthy – If we say we are trustworthy – Then others can say – They can trust us – That we are worthy of their trust – That they can talk to us – and in so doing – show us their vulnerable side – And we won't take advantage of that – They can share with us happenings in their <u>past</u> – and we won't use mistakes that they made – to control them in the <u>present</u>.

Responsible – Being a responsible person means <u>owning</u> our thoughts, feelings and acts – as they relate to the way we think, feel and act regarding our perceptions of and our interaction with others.

We don't react – and then present to others that they made us think, feel and act accordingly – Therefore we have little-to-no responsibility for our behavior – Nor the way things turned out for us or the other. We don't flip-flop nor project blame back onto the other – in order to exonerate ourselves from whatever the unfortunate outcome of our negative reciprocal interaction.

Dependable and Accountable tap into very similar kinds of promised behavior. The other can count on – Depend upon us – Count on and depend upon – go hand in hand – in assuring and insuring – that whatever is promised will happen. Lean on us – Let us worry about it – We won't let the other down – Promises made will be promises kept – We would tell the other if what they need from us is beyond what we are capable of doing for the other – We don't have to – We choose to. Rest easy – We say – We have things under control.

Truthful – When we are truthful – the other can take our word for it – Our word is as good as gold – Believe us when we tell you what we have to say is the truth – (So help us God). We will tell the other the truth – Even if – Or when – It puts us in a bad light.

If we are a loyal person – with the before-mentioned loyalty Qualities – and we present them for the other to perceive – The question is From Whence – From Whom – Did these Qualities derive?

What then is the ORIGIN of our Loyalty?

Hopefully we perceived these qualities in our Parent(s): In the way they treated each other – What they said to each other – How they said it – What they did for each other.

We perceived the way(s) – They Counted on – Relied upon – Trusted in – Depended upon each other – The way they spoke the Truth to each other – were Direct – Open – and Honest with each other.

Likewise, in the way they treated us – in giving us their word – and keeping it – Promises made were promises kept – They put our best interests first – They took such good care of us – Protected us – Showed us in so many ways – How much they loved us – They made us feel – that they were committed to making us feel – that we were very important to them – They did and said – what they could – to raise our self esteem and self worth.

For others of us the loyalty our Grandparent(s) showed us made the big difference in our lives – In those instances where our parents came up short in the love and loyalty department – Our grandparent(s) gloriously came through for us – and doing so – we felt loved by them and loyalty from them.

Friendships sometimes over time can promulgate loyalty – We say – over time – because they (friendships) need – opportunities of togetherness – to grow into a – mutual comingling – of reciprocal accountability and trust.

Family loyalty is fraught with uncertainties amongst family members – Uncertainties stemming from the comingling of unpredictable, idiosyncratic personality differences – When mom, dad, siblings interact – each with their own agenda.

Dissensions arise between family members – falling-outs – incongruent behaviors threaten the unity and solidarity of the family structure.

Individual loyalties are challenged by family loyalty concerns. The family struggles to keep family loyalty alive and well. This is no small task – as individual family members vacillate in their willingness to commit – i.e. to set aside personal desires and goals – "for the good of the family" as a whole.

For "the good of the family," family members may sacrifice their intentions to leave and branch out on their own – and instead stay – (at least for the foreseeable future) – in order to stabilize their family's core.

For "the good of the family" – When any of its members are threatened from outside sources – The family coalesces and shields and protects its family members.

Take on one family member – and one ends up taking on all family members. Such is the formidable reaction to the prospect of unwelcomed intrusion from the outside – Step up to challenge one of them – and the rest of the family is quick to close ranks.

Should we step out from our family – It's a whole other world out there. Since there are no guarantees – even within our own family structure – that loyalties will perpetually last – We may turn to others such as extended family members for their help and support – and build up relationships with the same – as we look for extended loyalty to sustain us – Grandparents, uncles, aunts, cousins all are potential loyalty prospects.

Again grandparents come to mind – Many of us have grateful reflections of how they stepped up to the plate and became our surrogates for loyalty.

Some of us learned – that we were loveable – from our grandparent(s) – With whom we spent an inordinate amount of time – experiencing the love and loyalty they offered us – With no strings attached – A love and loyalty that we could count upon without reservation.

At our grandparent(s) knee – We found comfort, solace and peace in their presence – and upon reflection – We remember How precious was their love – and How it eventually warmed our heart – enabling us to become <u>heart-warmers</u> ourselves.

<u>As a youngster</u> – Preteen or so – What loyalty we experienced – (if we did) – Came from our siblings – Siblings looking out for each other – Standing up for each other – Mutually demonstrating to each other – The strong bond that binds them.

<u>As teens</u> – Stretching our <u>circle of life</u> to include classmates and friends – Discovering (in some instances the hard way) – That life – outside the family – can sometimes become quite a challenge – as temporary relationships are made – and subsequently broken – as quickly as they are made.

<u>As young adults</u> – Our quest is/was for relationships that might last longer – and perhaps be more meaningful – We tended to look for more <u>similarities</u> than <u>differences</u> when making friends.

<u>As friends</u> – Like interests in – Common appetites for – Shared passions about – can often culminate in extended meaningful, close relationships – And within such friendships reciprocal loyalties abide

– Reciprocity is loyalty's best friend – Need a friend! – Be a friend!

Considering ourselves – introspectively and extrospectively – While giving credence to our origin of loyalty – (i.e. – from whence our loyalty derived – (if indeed it did)) – The How of how we became a loyal person – (if indeed we are) – We now are capable of <u>presenting ourselves as loyal</u>.

A Loyal Person Is As A Loyal Person Does

If being a loyal person for us is a personality priority we are then comfortable presenting loyalty as part of who we are – and what we are all about – In so doing we soon see how others are appreciatively drawn to it as an attribute they themselves may desire.

A loyal person <u>is</u> as a loyal person <u>does</u>. When interacting with an other we present perceptual cues that represent loyalty to them and perceive how they react – (remembering their reaction will be their presentation).

How the other responds to our perceptual cues of loyalty will give us insights about ourselves and about the perceiver regarding whether what we present (that we are – a loyal person) – is being perceived as such. The other's reaction goes a long way in validating this.

As we consider being a loyal person to an other – what questions should we be asking ourselves?

Some of our answers to ourselves will be based on what we have experienced before – (if indeed we have) – when we presented qualities of loyalty to the other. [Keep in mind that this is before we perceive the other as being loyal]…

Questions like:

- Do we believe that loyalty begets loyalty?
- What if we're loyal and the other is not?
- There's only so much loyalty to go around – What if being loyal so dominates our life that it leaves us with little time or energy for anything else – Is this a good thing for us?
- Is loyalty a weakness or a strength? [A weakness if it controls our life – or leads us to allow others to control our life.] – [A strength if we are in control of it.]
- When does loyalty become naïveté? – [When we are so needy we don't see what's coming.]
- Wasted loyalty – Is there such a thing? – [Not if we were the one who was loyal.]

- Can one have too much loyalty? – [If our need to be loyal is too large it makes us vulnerable to other's manipulations.]
- Who determines whether our loyalty is excessive? – [Ultimately, we do – Ultimately we realize our loyalty is one-way – We're the Giver – The other the Taker.]
- Does the one to whom we are loyal have a part in this? – [Of course – especially if they're primarily a Taker and thus reinforce our too-large-a-need-to-be-loyal.]

Even as we own our need to be loyal – we readdress our thoughts and feelings about where loyalty rates in our repertoire of positive traits – It's right up there at the top of our hierarchy of needs – Thus we rise to answer questions about its relevancy and importance in our lives.

- Is loyalty an admirable quality? – [Yes.]
- Is it a noble quality? – [Yes, the noblest of all human virtues.]
- Is it a quality for fools? – [We think not.]
- For dreamers? – [We think not.]

- Is it a quality that has <u>outlived</u> its <u>relevancy</u>? – [We think not.]

- In this day and age can we <u>afford</u> to be loyal – mentally, financially, socially, personally? [This is a very subjective question with multi-parts – To be answered by each of us according to the relative importance loyalty has for us – to be the loyal person we are. Some may conclude we can't afford <u>not</u> to be a loyal person. The price to our self concept and self worth would be too high.]

All of this suggests that each of us – (maybe without realizing it) – tends to – (within ourselves) – construct a <u>Hierarchy</u> for Loyalty – A rank ordering – (if you will) – of whom we look to for <u>reciprocal loyalty</u>. There are <u>Levels</u> of Loyalty – and accordingly <u>Degrees</u> of Loyalty – effected by the kind of relationship we're talking about…

- Question: Would we expect the same kind – and degree – of loyalty from an acquaintance – friend – close friend –

relative – immediate family member – spouse?

- Have we friends who are more loyal than family members? – [Yes, indeed this may be the case – Greater loyalty from one – Lesser from the other. <u>Each</u> of us needs to answer this according to our <u>own</u> <u>experiences</u>.]

- What does "What have we done for the other lately" – have to say about Reciprocal Loyalty? – [That the Other's a Taker not a Giver]

- Can one be a <u>little bit</u> loyal? – [No more than one can be a little bit pregnant.]

- How far does our loyalty take us? – Our answer probably rests upon to whom we're being loyal and of course whether the loyalty is reciprocal. [We'll get to this later when we specifically address the <u>nature</u> of <u>our primary relationship</u> – (if we have or had – or hope to have one) – as it relates to reciprocal loyalty.]

- Does it make sense to be loyal to someone – before we know whether they are loyal to us? – [Who should go <u>first</u> – We or the Other?] – This is a good entré to what we should look for in <u>sizing up</u> whether the other is loyal – (especially if we are considering entering a primary relationship with them – (if we are).

But before we look specifically for loyalty in our primary relationship we need to address the subject of <u>what</u> we look for – <u>In General</u> – in a person to determine whether the other is a loyal person or not – The answer is obvious. We look for <u>perceptual cues</u> – i.e. aspects of person perception regarding the other's presentation – <u>How</u> they <u>say</u> – <u>what</u> they <u>say</u> – but primarily <u>how</u> they <u>act</u> – i.e. the acts they present verbally and nonverbally.

But first we've got to get to know them – (over time – and take our time with this) – We find out what they have to say about loyalty and the qualities that comprise it – We assert – They reply. We ask for – They supply – What more to ask – What more to know

– Primarily we get to know them by their acts – ["By their fruits we shall know them."]

We get to know them by observing <u>what</u> and <u>how</u> they <u>present</u> the <u>qualities</u> of <u>loyalty</u> (<u>trustworthy</u>, <u>dependable</u>, <u>responsible</u>, <u>accountable</u>, <u>truthful</u>) – Using <u>person perception</u> and <u>self experience</u> that's how we get to know them – and they, us. We also get to know how they perceive us – and they get to know how we perceive them. [By <u>extrospection</u>.] – Each of us, get to know ourselves regarding our loyalty-ness – by lowering our defenses – and by going <u>inside</u> ourselves (<u>introspection</u>).

In these relationships – other than our primary relationship – if we're fortunate – we may find loyalty in the other – and the other may find loyalty in us – for the other – This is a very good thing – Especially if this experience turns out to be a precursor to our finding the one with whom we will have a primary relationship – We will know <u>what</u> to <u>look</u> for in the <u>other</u> and <u>ourselves</u> with respect to the <u>existence</u> and <u>essence</u> of <u>reciprocal loyalty</u>.

Speaking Now Of Our Primary Relationship

Speaking now of our primary relationship – (Some of us are thinking – Finally we're getting to our primary relationship!) – We are going to be looking for (perceiving) in ourselves and our other <u>all</u> the <u>loyalty qualities</u> we may have previously experienced <u>outside</u> our primary relationship – <u>Plus</u> <u>Love</u>, <u>Commitment</u> and <u>Truthfulness</u>.

Plus Love

Love which comingles with loyalty in our primary relationship is typically <u>not</u> present in our relationship with (let's say) a good friend. Of course some of us can attest to the fact that in our case it was our "good friend" that we ultimately fell in love with. Keep in mind though that for the rest of us who engaged in reciprocal loyalty with our good friend – but stopped short of loving them – that this doesn't for a moment disparage them – or our loyalty to them – nor their loyalty to us.

In our <u>Permanent Primary Relationship</u> with the other – each of us must deem ourselves – and the other – as capable of both Love and Loyalty – and be presenting to each other perceptual cues – that we can reciprocally verify this is so. This is what we and the other need from each other to go forward together.

Whether we have had a primary relationship – that didn't work out – where there was plenty of blame to go around – Or we sadly have lost our loved one in death – are missing them terribly – and are struggling with the pros and cons of living alone – Or perhaps after giving it time – are at least considering another primary relationship – Or we are looking to have our first primary relationship – Or we are looking to shore up the one we have – There will be plenty for us to learn – digest – gain insight from – and hopefully make <u>Behavioral Changes</u>.

Once again there are a lot of questions we will try to answer as our <u>Quest for Loyalty</u> now includes Love as well.

Love And Loyalty – How Do The Two Relate?

LOVE = Feelings, sensations, thoughts – When we perceive our other – Feelings of warmth, of desire

– of wanting to get closer – wanting to touch – yearning to hold. Heart feelings of how much we love them – of how special they are.

Heart feelings of Cherishing – Like we can't get enough of our other – Like we want to hold onto the other – Like we want to get as close as we can to the other – And never let go.

Is it love or loyalty that initially attracts? – Often love comes first in the early stages of a primary relationship. When we're "in love" this tends to take over our thoughts and feelings. The reality that we are experiencing such love-thoughts and feelings – when we are with the other – (or for that matter even when we're not with the other) – tends to grab our attention and restrict our looking any deeper for the presence of loyalty in the other's actions.

Love often captivates our thoughts and feelings – so that acts that follow (that may in fact be acts of loyalty – that the other is presenting) – may go unrecognized as such by us – or the other – If what is happening to us feels good, to us or the other – That's all that matters.

Thus Love and Loyalty <u>come together</u> and become the beginning foundation of our primary relationship.

Since the subject of this book is Loyalty – (albeit we have acknowledged that Love cannot be denied its importance as well) – We need to ask more questions about their <u>respective relevancy</u> as they relate to the <u>substance</u> and <u>sustenance</u> of our <u>primary relationship</u>.

Can we start out by agreeing that both Love and Loyalty are <u>undeniably essential</u> to the <u>psychological health</u> and <u>well being</u> of our <u>primary relationship</u>?

Can we say that Loyalty is <u>more essential</u> than Love is – Or that Love is <u>more essential</u> than Loyalty is? At this juncture this would be difficult for us to say either way.

Incidentally, the <u>dictionary</u> which doesn't deal with constructs <u>defines</u> Loyalty as Faithfulness. [But let's not get ahead of ourselves with respect to the order of things – and thus imagine that one can exist without the other in our primary relationship.]

Whether Love <u>comes before</u> Loyalty or Loyalty <u>comes before</u> Love – <u>Neither one can come before</u> and <u>be the same</u> as they are "<u>Post-Commitment.</u>" [This is because Faithfulness is not required <u>before</u> Commitment but only <u>after</u>.]

Love and Loyalty are both very different when experienced <u>outside</u> our primary relationship – since Love then is mostly <u>Thoughts</u> and <u>Feelings</u> and "<u>Loyalty Acts</u>" of <u>Trustworthiness</u>, <u>Accountability</u> and <u>Truthfulness</u>.

Love And Loyalty Inside Our Primary Relationship

The designation <u>Primary</u> speaks to the <u>Specialness</u>, <u>Uniqueness</u>, <u>One-of-a-kind-ness</u> of the relationship into which we are bringing and subsequently seeking the qualities of <u>Love</u> and <u>Loyalty</u>, <u>Commitment</u> and <u>Faithfulness</u>.

Our primary relationship is the one – (and often only) – relationship that we allow ourselves to believe – (have faith in) – the presence of – and the practice of – Reciprocal Loyalty and Faithfulness.

The primary relationship which we have – or hope to have – begins with an emphasis on thoughts and feelings we have for the other – At the risk of oversimplifying the process of establishing and perpetuating our primary relationship – let us agree to say that in its earliest stages – thoughts and feelings about the acts we present and perceive – (i.e. reciprocal acts we perceive) – take over and predominate – And by the same token an analysis of the meaning and origin of these acts gets very little perceptual attention. [Without coming right out and saying it – What we are in essence alluding to is our tendency <u>Not</u> To "Look Before We Leap!"]

Small wonder then for us <u>Love</u> (with all its warmth in our thoughts and feelings) <u>came first</u>. Love which is more a <u>state</u> of thoughts, words and feelings than a <u>presentation</u> of – and an <u>analysis</u> of – acts (even if they be in reality Acts of Love (or Acts of Loyalty, or Both)). – Which is to say we love a person for the way thoughts about them make us feel – and for how they make us feel – when we are actually with them – (or even when we're not with them).

All of this is leading up to say that Love (whose essence appears to be indefinable) while experientially wonderful must ultimately be grounded in the realities of observable behaviors that more than just accompany Love – Define it by its actions.

Thus Loyalty and all its loving qualities becomes an integral part of the relationship between Love and Loyalty in a reciprocal primary relationship.

To speak of Love and Loyalty in the same breath is to underscore their singular and mutual importance to the status, significance, stability and security within one's Primary Relationship.

Love and Loyalty don't automatically come together in the same package. Either one, however, can start the ball rolling. If Love starts up a primary relationship and gets it going – Can Loyalty be far behind? – We don't know for sure – We can't know for sure – We would surely like to think so – But thinking so – Doesn't make it so!

Love has a tendency to get ahead of Loyalty in a primary relationship. That's probably because we tend to lead with our feelings and feelings tend to influence thoughts and <u>both</u> feelings and thoughts influence our perceptions – Resulting in our seeing what we <u>want</u> to see – And thus we can end up <u>misperceiving what's really there</u>!

Loyalty on the other hand is much more <u>concretized</u> in <u>perceptual acts</u>. Thus Loyalty in the other is <u>easier</u> to perceive in their <u>observable acts</u> – Acts which present Qualities of Loyalty presented in a Loving way – Thus bringing Love and Loyalty together (<u>seemingly</u>, but not necessarily <u>surely</u>).

"Seemingly" suggests the possibility of <u>misperceiving</u> the <u>meaning</u> and <u>intention</u> of what we <u>perceptually judge</u> to be the "<u>Whole Package</u>" (Of Love <u>and</u> Loyalty, that is).

Commitment And Faithfulness

Lest we be discouraged from the start – Remember – This we can get better at with <u>practice</u> – I.e. perceiving what is really there and not just what we want or wish were there.

All of this takes time and practice – Believing that through person perception and self experience we may become more astute in getting to know Our Real Selves and in getting to know the Real Self of Our Other.

"What you see is what you get" – [Where have we heard this before?] – Really?! – What we get is what the other presents – And what the other presents is a function of what their personality has to offer us.

Reciprocally two persons – two personalities present – react – and present back. The more each person in their primary relationship gets in touch with their <u>Real Self</u> – (having lowered their defenses) – and presents accordingly – The more we can trust (and they as well) that what each of us perceives in the other is the Real Deal!

The more and better we get to know our other – and our other – us – (know in the sense that each of us has lowered our defenses – (thus knowing ourselves better and they knowing themselves better)) the more confident each of us can be when we mutually decide to make a Commitment to each other – Commitment at the time we make it – Of a Lifetime – For a Lifetime.

Commitment … Without the Commitment – it's all just "Smoke and Mirrors." Therefore we ask – What does it mean for us (to us) to make this Commitment to each other?

The Commitment – The Pledge – The Promise Above All Promises – To be with each other – and love each other – and be loyal to each other – until one or the other – or both of us – leave this earth (humanly speaking).

The Road To Commitment is a metaphor for how we experience it – Curves and bumps – ups and downs – detours – under construction – one-ways – even seemingly dead ends at times – [Sounds like a description of things to come] – Thusly Love and Loyalty

35

are essential for "the Drive." Back to the beginning – To quote my own words from my book *Closeness Without Control*: Two persons, two personalities meet – They begin a relationship – If that relationship becomes more than just a passing fancy – If the two are seriously perpetuating the relationship – and they both have a vested interest in doing so – A Committed Relationship ensues. The committed relationship may be in the context of <u>marriage</u> – of <u>living together</u> – or even <u>living apart</u> – But nevertheless committed.

<u>Commitment</u> is the key that opens the door for Loyalty and Faithfulness to enter.

<u>Faithfulness</u> – That's the <u>quality</u> – The <u>attribute</u> that is <u>valued</u> the <u>most</u> by the <u>two</u> who are in a primary relationship.

When one is in a primary relationship with their other – in which the two are committed – then Faithfulness in that relationship is a <u>prerequisite</u> for Loyalty in that relationship.

Faithful = Full of Faith in Self and in the Other.

Believing in One's Self. Believing in the Other's Self.

Have Faith in = Believe in.

Believing in One's Self means we can be one to have Faith in. I can have Faith in My Self.

The Other can have Faith in Their Self and I can have Faith in Their Self.

But – And that's a Big But – I and the other are only human – Imperfect at times – Unworthy of the other's believing in me – And I in them.

The affirmation of our human-ness makes believing in ourselves and the other challenging and problematic – but convincingly possible.

I have Faith in Myself that I can do this – Included in the this – of course – are the other Attributes – Qualities of Loyalty.

You have Faith in Your Self that You can do this –

We can do this – We can be this – For ourselves and each other.

Once Loyalty and Faithfulness are mutually recognized and verified by each in themselves and the other then the impetus to bear witness to their present and future existence and essence (much more often than not) – leads the couple to <u>pledge</u> the same Loyalty and Faithfulness – along with <u>other invaluable qualities</u> such as – To <u>Love</u> and to <u>Cherish</u>.

The <u>human</u> factor which is inextricably inherent in our Pledge motivates most of us to make our Pledge before <u>God</u> and <u>Supportive Witnesses</u>.

The <u>recognition</u> and <u>acceptance</u> of the <u>limitations</u> of one's <u>ability</u> and <u>propensity</u> to love and cherish – to be loyal and faithful no matter what – If left wholly and purely to our own devices – We'd come up significantly short so… That's why People of Faith or people who desire to be People of Faith (I.e. more than they are at present) – Choose to ask a Servant of God to lead them in the Pledge of Love, Loyalty and Faithfulness.

Before God and witnesses – (<u>God</u> would be <u>there</u> anyway) – But this is to reinforce the couple's belief and conviction – that <u>He</u> is there and that the couple is committing to Him – as well as each other – That they will keep their Pledge (so help us God).

Faithful to God is one thing – Faithfulness to One Another is another thing.

If one is Faithful to God is it a <u>Given</u> that one will be Faithful to the other? A "given" is perhaps saying too much – ("given" – "To err is human") – "Given" would suggest to some that loving – cherishing – being loyal and faithful to the other – are God-bestowed – I.e. that these are gifts from God that He gives to us – to give to ourselves and each other.

Our faith in God <u>enables</u> us to be faithful to God and faithful to each other.

God says – Be faithful to Me and I will give you the Crown of Life.

He asks us to be faithful to each other until death do us part.

Do we see how these two go together? – Faithful to God until death – Faithful to each other until death. Faithful to God – Therefore faithful to each other – Would that this be so – That the one would <u>automatically follow</u> the other – Not so – Loyalty, Faithfulness, Love are <u>human</u> attributes – which <u>unless practiced</u> there's <u>no</u> <u>guarantee</u> they'll <u>last</u>. They must be <u>presented</u> and <u>experienced</u> to be perceived for what they are – And ultimately come to mean – to us – and our other – To be fair about it – (Keeping in mind one's human frailty) – On the one hand we say that even if we count God in our future plans – Faithfulness to ourselves and each other – until death parts us – Is "no given" – And on the other hand – If God is not part of the picture of how we proceed with each other – It still is possible that we could be faithful to ourselves and each other throughout our lives – (Possible, yes – But – (question) – Should we bet ours – and our other's life on it – (just saying!)). If before God and witnesses we pledge our Faithfulness and our Love and Loyalty until the end – What are our chances of "pulling this off" – [Let each of us answer this question for ourselves.] – What is the <u>State of our Affairs</u>? – This begs the question: What is the "<u>State of our Affairs</u>" – [In some ways an unfortunate choice of words] – If our thoughts immediately jump to that which perhaps above all others threatens the "<u>State of our Affairs</u>" – Which is <u>meant to refer to the state, the condition – the well-being – of our committed primary relationship</u>.

"State Of Our Affairs"

We need to examine ourselves – Vis a vis our other – And our other – Vis a vis ourselves – With regard to our perception of ourselves – Our perception of our other – Our perception of how the other perceives us –

And their perception of how we perceive them – [Whew! – Enough of these perceptions already.]

After all this perceiving has been going on – At some point – (If both of us are willing) – We'll share with each other our perceptions, thoughts and feelings about how we are doing – And what each of us thinks might be <u>good the way it is – and</u> what we (hopefully agree) may <u>need some changing</u>.

What will come under our <u>careful caring examination</u> will be what we <u>committed to from the start</u> – I.e. Love, Loyalty and Faithfulness.

Faithfulness

[First of all – we have not named these three in order of their importance to us. Each of us – individually – will decide this for ourselves.] – To some of us – (perhaps many of us) – Love is most important – To others of us – Loyalty with all its accompanying attributes – (Trustworthy, Responsible, Dependable, Accountable, Truthful) is most important. Faithfulness – which although it defines Loyalty – And thus we could say is the most important part of it – seems to stand alone – (in a class by itself – And seems to be the one standard –

above all others – That is used to judge whether or not
we are <u>keeping our mutual commitment (I.e. to Love, be
Loyal and Faithful to each other)</u>.

In our primary relationship then we commit to each other that we will love, be loyal, and especially be faithful to each other for as long as we live – To give us a clearer picture of what we hope to see – (both in ourselves and our other) – as we strive to be the kind of person who can love – be loyal and – above all – be faithful to the other, – we need to consider <u>subjectively what objectively a psychologically healthy and well-lived reciprocal primary relationship of love, loyalty and faithfulness looks like</u>.

We begin then with what reciprocal loving in our primary relationship might look like – If it is indeed happening – Or if not – We can strive to make it happen – Note: To those of us who perchance have read my first book (*Closeness Without Control* – "The key to a loving reciprocal relationship of assertive independent equals") – The following may be familiar to us – But hopefully we would agree well worth revisiting.

Loving – Clearly loving and closeness are parts of each other. [Here comes what I like to refer to as a "Fischerism"…<u>To be love-able one must first be loveable</u> – the Order in which <u>Becoming</u> Loving occurs.] – So for us in a primary relationship the hope is that someone in our <u>past</u> – or the one in our <u>present</u> – has gotten through to us – <u>That We're Loveable</u>. This is critical to our Capacity for Closeness – Both to <u>Receive it</u> and <u>Give it</u> – That we <u>perceive ourselves as loveable</u>.

To achieve closeness with our other we need to become <u>more assertive</u> with each other. <u>To Be Assertive</u> means that we first <u>identify</u> what we <u>need</u> (more love, more closeness) – And then <u>pursue it</u>. It means <u>being responsible</u> for what we <u>think</u>, <u>feel</u>, <u>say</u> and <u>do</u>. It means being <u>direct</u>, <u>open</u> and <u>honest</u> about what we're <u>thinking</u>, <u>feeling</u> and <u>needing</u>.

Two people embarking on a journey of <u>Heightened Closeness</u> must of one accord believe the journey is worth taking. As <u>life</u> itself is a <u>process</u> <u>not</u> an <u>end</u> – So is <u>closeness</u> a <u>process</u> – That has <u>no end</u> until we <u>are no more</u> – Once we decide it's a journey worth taking – An effort worth making – We need to become <u>proactive</u> – Willing to experiment – Try new behaviors –

Take risks – Confront anxieties – Challenge avoidant tendencies.

Above all – <u>Trust Each Other</u> – [Here we overlap with loyalty]. Trust = An exchange of vulnerabilities without either taking advantage of the other – [Another "Fischerism"] – Indeed, as we <u>make exchanges</u> that will help us <u>get</u> closer and <u>stay</u> closer, we will be <u>exposing</u> our <u>most vulnerable selves</u>.

In a <u>loving</u>, <u>reciprocal</u> relationship we are on <u>both</u> the <u>giving</u> and <u>receiving end</u> of closeness. We may be more <u>comfortable</u> on one end than the other. Our <u>challenge</u> then will be to <u>try</u> the end that tends to <u>peak</u> our <u>anxiety</u>. Our other can help us <u>gradually desensitize</u> ourselves to those <u>situations</u> that make us <u>uncomfortable</u> – If we are more comfortable hugging than being hugged, our Soul Mate needs to be gentle – But keep hugging us <u>despite</u> our stiffness and lack of responsiveness.

Another example of our willingness to change – in order to experience more closeness with our other – would be whether or not we <u>say yes</u> to doing something that our <u>loved one</u> is <u>interested in</u> and <u>enjoys</u> – (Whereas we couldn't <u>care less</u>) – The important thing is when we say yes – "We're In" – We don't go kicking and screaming – We <u>open</u> ourselves to the experience – which then will <u>add to</u> rather than <u>subtract from</u> – the closeness of our <u>together-experience</u>. (Chalk up another one for <u>reciprocal love</u> and <u>closeness</u>.)

The aforementioned examples of how we achieve closeness, expressions of love and intimacy have left us without yet addressing the <u>potentially most heightened experience</u> of <u>closeness, love and intimacy</u> in our primary relationship – That would be <u>Sexual Intimacy</u>.

But hold on – One more experience – (or experiment if we prefer) – to cover that we might try – (if "we're game") – to heighten our closeness – and that is <u>Allocentric Perception</u> – as it relates to <u>experiencing</u> each other <u>as much as possible</u> but <u>stopping short of sexual intimacy</u> . . . We pick a time and place in our home where we feel most comfortable and have optimal privacy – Again, to experience each other as much as possible we will use <u>Allocentric Perception</u> – (not <u>Autocentric Perception</u> – which refers to experiencing one's human or physical environment with one sense only – Ex. Touching a rose uses our tactile sense).

Allocentric Perception – on the other hand – is engaging our human or physical environment with as many of our senses possible – To touch a rose – taste a rose – smell a rose – move a rose through the air – see a rose – Whatever sense(s) we decide to start out with – We should go slowly – Take our time – Not be in a hurry – Get as much out of the experience as we can.

Concentrating on our <u>tactile sense</u> – Each of us with the tips of our fingers – running them gently up and down our other's bare back, chest or breast – We're not talking massaging here – We're talking ever so gently stroking each other.

Here again Reciprocity is vital to the experience. <u>Giving</u> and <u>receiving sensation</u> are two very distinctive experiences – Touch a rose – Let a rose touch you – We're also talking about <u>persevering</u> when stroking. A <u>quick pass</u> over the area will surely be perceived as <u>less than enthusiastic</u>.

Some of our other senses are addressed when we fill the air with the aroma of scented candles – Or the burning of incense – Listen to music that soothes and relaxes us – Lying side by side on our backs – smelling –

listening – relaxing – feeling <u>tension moving out</u> of our bodies.

Or we can get naked – and hold each other like a spoon on a spoon – taking turns with who puts their arms around whom – There's nothing like it – There's nothing like skin-on-skin – The warmth passing back and forth between bodies – It's like the two of us are in a world of our own – We feel completely safe, secure – and as close as we can be.

Taking a bath with each other – Facing each other – Or straddling each other – Rinsing each other – Having candles lighted along the side of the tub – Wine, apples and cheese – at arm's length.

The question arises when we are engaging in these kind of behaviors <u>will this lead</u> us from <u>general</u> closeness to <u>sexual</u> closeness? – It may – It may not. If things are moving in that direction – and both – <u>or one</u> – <u>of you</u> don't want to go there – That's where <u>assertiveness</u> comes in – <u>Each</u> needs to let the <u>other</u> <u>know</u> whether <u>sexual arousal</u> is occurring during this <u>exercise</u> of <u>love</u> and <u>closeness</u> – If <u>both of us</u> want to go there – No need to stop – or change direction – <u>Otherwise</u>, <u>go back</u> to stroking and touching – that promulgates feelings and sensations of love and closeness – But not arousal.

As long as we're alluding to sexual intimacy and closeness – (where both of us are wanting that) – it seems that the Foreplay portion of the sexual experience has pretty much the same components we talked about when we interact with each other – using most of our senses – The main difference is that here our intention is to arouse and bring the other to experience that specific kind of love and closeness.

In the Foreplay mode – our mental, emotional and physical parts of ourselves combine with one goal in mind – To bring our other and ourselves to a special heightened sense of love and closeness – Along with arousal – If the other in our primary relationship doesn't feel loveable in our presence – then we need to do all we can – (provided that we feel loveable ourselves) – to warm them up with our warmth – We need to hang in there – It may take a while but it will happen – And when it does the closeness and love we yearn for from them will occur.

Our love needs to be reciprocal. Two loveables reciprocating that love will keep the closeness growing.

We warm them up – They warm us up – They warm us up – We warm them up – Back and forth we go – No one is keeping track of who goes first – The important thing is that the love and closeness are <u>reciprocal</u> – flowing from each to each. <u>One-way</u> loving, <u>one-way</u> closeness will not do. To keep them <u>going</u> and <u>growing</u> they must be <u>two-way</u>!

Each of us experiences the act of Sexual Intercourse in our own <u>very personal</u> and <u>private way</u>. It is something that we experience but can't find the words to sufficiently describe. With <u>sensations</u> at their <u>peak</u> we are <u>overwhelmed</u> by them and the <u>experience takes over</u> the <u>two</u> who are <u>experiencing</u> it.

The <u>After-Glow experience</u> – Our sensations have peaked – The release – The relief have come – Calmness has been restored – We are left experiencing the <u>aftermath</u> of that which we <u>individually</u> and <u>collectively</u> enjoyed – And then, in some <u>inexplicable way</u> – If we just let it happen – Our love and closeness is <u>heightened</u> in a <u>relaxing</u>, <u>comfortable</u> and <u>caring way</u>.

This is <u>no time</u> to <u>roll over</u> – And <u>turn away</u> – Or <u>get up</u> – And <u>rush to wash away</u> the <u>remnants</u> of our <u>close encounter</u>. It is a time <u>to stay</u> – If not to <u>hold</u> –

Then lie spread-eagled on our backs – <u>basking</u> in the warmth of love and closeness – that still remains – in an even <u>stronger</u> – and <u>more noticeable</u> way – within us.

Love as depicted in our examples speaks to <u>its</u> <u>specialness</u> as it brings us together to <u>reciprocally share</u> its <u>opportunities</u> and <u>experiences</u> which <u>magnify</u> our <u>love</u> and <u>closeness</u> and <u>verify</u> the <u>"one and only"</u> nature of our <u>commitment</u> to each other – It is through <u>acts of</u> <u>reciprocal loving</u> that we achieve and enjoy <u>peaks</u> of <u>closeness</u> that are <u>indigenous only</u> to our <u>very personal</u> and <u>private mutually shared experiences</u>.

What If We Can't Have Both?

Such love experiences we cherish as do we the one with whom we share these same experiences within the context of our loving reciprocal primary relationship – Our <u>commitment</u> then is to be <u>loving</u> and <u>loyal</u> to our primary other <u>for as long as we live</u> – Love and Loyalty – we are committed to in our primary relationship.

The question that we need to ask ourselves and answer for ourselves – But not for our other – is – Which is more important to us and for us – To us – As we consider <u>what's going on inside of us</u> – For us as we consider what we're looking for from our other – Which would we choose assuming they were mutually exclusive? – Love or Loyalty? – Either way our lives together would be dramatically different and incomplete with one – But not the other.

Consider the following statements made – and ponder their relevancy – as we examine our own primary relationship – What would our primary relationship be like should either Love or Loyalty be missing?:

- Loyalty is a <u>validation</u> of loving. [I can tell that you love me because you are loyal to me.]
- If we <u>truly</u> love – We will be loyal too – ["Truly" is the operative word]
- Love without loyalty is an oxymoron [What more is there to say!]
- Loyalty can exist without love [But is its <u>essence</u> there, if not then what?]
- I love you – But [What's the "But" about? – Here it comes!]
- What I love about you is your loyalty and all that it entails – [OK! Sounds good!]
- Love and disloyalty cannot coexist [They can – But should they? What has changed?]
- I can still be loyal to you – But I don't love you anymore – [What's wrong with this picture?]

- The thing I love most about you is your loyalty – First to me – Then to others – (albeit to a lesser degree). [You've got company – A lot of us feel this way!]

- How could you do what you did and <u>still claim</u> you love me – That I'm the only one you love – That you couldn't live without me! [The "How could You!" underscores the gravity of the <u>acts of betrayal</u> rendering <u>meaningless</u> the <u>words</u> and <u>promises</u> that <u>came before them</u>.]

- I can't love someone I can't count on. [Suggests Counting On is high in the hierarchy of what one needs from the other.]

- I can't love someone who isn't truthful, responsible, dependable, trustworthy [All these are qualities that add up to the other <u>missing loyalty from the other</u>.]

- You have all the attributes of loyalty but there is something missing – Could it be that I don't love you anymore. [I need more from you than loyalty – I'm not feeling the love from you – Therefore none for you.]

- You're <u>more loyal</u> to your: <u>mother</u>, <u>father</u>, <u>child</u>, <u>family</u>, <u>employer</u> than you are to <u>me</u>! – [I feel left out – Bringing up the rear – You're just not here when I need you – When you are here it's just like you're not here.]

- One thing I'll never do is <u>lie</u> to you. [You're saying that you will always tell me truth. "One thing" – Are there other things you will do to me?]

- If everyone else lets you down, I will never let you down – [You're saying that you will <u>always</u> – Again, I can believe or not – my choice!]

- I'll always be there whenever you need me. [Words! – <u>Proof</u> of the <u>pudding</u> is the <u>eating thereof</u>.]

- I'm glad we're best friends and not just lovers – [You are my best friend – I do love you – And know you love me.]

- I will never leave you nor forsake you. [The word "never" – Absolutely?!]

- You are my one and only – [What am I the one and only of? – Or for?]

- We were meant for each other – [Meaning what?]

- God meant for us to be together – [This certainly could have been the case.]

- Promises made are promises kept – [One would hope so.]

- Forever loving you – [My personal favorite – I sign all the cards I give to <u>my other</u> like this.]

- No matter what – You'll always be true to me – [I see you as truthful – I speak for you.]

- One thing I don't have to worry about is that there is – Or will be – Someone else in our present or future – [Not to worry – On what do we base this? – Not to worry – Ourselves – Both of us – The other's Self.]

As we perused our possible (hopefully so) <u>experiences of reciprocal love</u> within our primary relationship we were struck by the <u>specialness</u> of Loving and Being Loved and realized how much we <u>yearned</u> for it and <u>appreciated</u> it when we <u>experienced</u> it.

A closer look at Loyalty and what it means to us – That we are both at the giving and receiving end of it – Should put us in a better position to answer the question before us – Which would we choose – If Love and Loyalty were mutually exclusive – And therefore, we had to decide which one was <u>more important</u> to us? (And <u>go with that</u>?)

Sometimes Loving Acts are Loyal Acts and sometimes Loyal acts are Loving acts – If we had only one – We'd be missing the other one.

- You are the love of my life – Now and always – [That's how I feel – That's how I see you feel – That's how <u>I</u> feel <u>you</u> feel.]

So with all of these samples of how Love and Loyalty may interact in one's primary relationship – We've got a lot to think about regarding what's <u>going</u>

<u>on</u> in our primary relationship – Or for that matter what's <u>not going on</u> in our primary relationship – (That we wish it were).

Per usual, we'll be looking at ourselves – At our other – At how we reciprocally look to each other – In order to <u>gain insights</u> and <u>make behavioral changes</u> – If need be – But there will be one very <u>significant change</u> in <u>how we proceed</u> – From now on the <u>focus</u> will be on You – On Each of You Regarding what's going on in Your Primary Relationship – The <u>one assumption</u> that will need to be made – Is that You are in a <u>committed relationship</u> – (As we get up close and personal). Hopefully You will – (i.e. Both of You) be taking the <u>Litmus Test</u> that's offered – That will help <u>Each</u> of You decide <u>where You Both</u> are <u>regarding your quest</u> for <u>Reciprocal Love</u>, <u>Loyalty</u> and <u>Faithfulness</u>.

What's happening these days in your primary relationship regarding Love, Loyalty and Faithfulness? Let each of you answer this in your own way. [From here on in we're going to be lumping Love, Loyalty (with all its other attributes) and Faithfulness – (Conceding that Faithfulness seems generally

perceived to be the <u>most compelling and
consequential attribute propelling and preserving our
Reciprocal Commitment</u>).

The <u>one unknown</u> (and it's a Big One) – If one is looking to help you help yourselves in analyzing the status of your relationship – Is how each of you are <u>thinking</u> and <u>feeling about</u> – And <u>subjectively perceiving what's going on</u> in Your relationship.

[Note: Since my book's title is *Lamenting the Loss of Loyalty* – The rest of my book will be focusing on Loyalty – As it <u>specifically applies</u> to Faithfulness – And Faithfulness as it <u>specifically applies</u> to Loyalty. I <u>need to do this primarily because</u> of the <u>well-held tenet</u> that <u>Faithfulness only pertains to whether or not either one of us</u> [has <u>breached</u> the <u>sanctity</u> of our <u>committed primary relationship by having sexual relations with someone other than our other</u> (With whom we promised "<u>Never To Do</u>" until death parted us)]

If Loyalty expectations are that you can <u>trust</u> your other – That your other <u>will act responsibly</u> – That you can <u>depend on</u> your other – That you can <u>count on</u> your other to do what your other says they <u>will do</u> (and <u>not do</u>) – That your other will <u>always</u> tell you the truth – No matter what – And the Big One – That your other will <u>always be faithful</u> to you. [This begs the question – <u>How</u> are <u>you doing</u> so far?? Just askin'.]

Caveat (lest you forget) – This is also how <u>You promised to be</u> in Your <u>together-reciprocally committed relationship</u>! – FAITHFULNESS = Bond of Loyalty – Loyalty (especially with its most important component – Faithfulness) presupposes a <u>Bond between the two of you to be</u>…– Faithful to oneself to be Faithful to the other – Faithful to the other and Faithful to one's Self to be Faithful to the other's Self…

Questions:

- Can <u>one break</u> the bond? [It only <u>takes one</u>.]
- Can <u>there be</u> a bond if <u>one breaks</u> it? [Bond takes <u>two</u> – <u>One</u> won't do.]
- Once the bond is <u>broken</u> – Can it be <u>restored</u>? [Takes <u>one</u> to <u>break</u> it but <u>two</u> to <u>restore</u> it.]
- It takes <u>two</u> to <u>make</u> the bond but <u>only one</u> to <u>break</u> it. [Takes <u>two</u> to <u>make</u> it, only <u>one</u> to <u>break</u> it.]

- If <u>one breaks</u> the bond can the <u>other walk away without impunity</u>? [What about Reciprocal Responsibility – How does that factor in?]

Examples of <u>Bond Breakers</u>??... – [What breaks the bond – Disloyalty?] – What About DISLOYALTY?!...

What <u>constitutes</u> disloyalty? [Only unfaithfulness?]

[Disloyalty = "<u>Dissing</u>" loyalty – That's what we're doing when we're being disloyal – (I.e. we're dissing loyalty – (<u>Dismissing</u> it as it were – Like it doesn't matter – Like we could "give a rat's behind" about it).]

Disloyalty – An action always? – [You start it.]

A reaction sometimes? – [You're better than this.]

If your disloyalty is an action – [You started it]

If your disloyalty is a reaction – [The other started it.]

You did it – I did it – I did it – You did it – Disloyalty begets disloyalty! – [Nobody's left to pick up the pieces.]

If your disloyalty is a reaction – Does this really make a difference? – [The other starts it – You finish it – Two wrongs don't make it right.]

If a reaction to the other's action – Does this make your disloyalty any less? – [The other started – You finished – Both responses – Yours no less]

Especially is the aforementioned true if we're talking about <u>each</u> of <u>you</u> having a <u>sexual relationship with another outside your committed primary relationship</u> – So then what might be the <u>motivation</u> for this <u>particular brand of reciprocal disloyalty</u>? [These probably amount to "<u>plausible reasons</u>" in <u>defense</u> of <u>one's actions</u>]:

- <u>Get back</u> at the other
- The <u>other has been</u> disloyal
- The other is <u>unworthy</u> of our loyalty
- The other <u>doesn't appreciate</u> our loyalty

[We call these "plausible reasons" to underscore How High Our Defenses would be for one to rationalize one's behavior in this way. Despite the understanding of others and empathy from those – Who have been there – Done that – We must own our own choices!]

Defenses are at their all time high when we or one is having an affair. [In defense of ourselves.] – Maybe also when our other is having an affair. [In defense of the other and ourselves.] – The reality that one would choose to match the kind of disloyalty of their other with their own act of unfaithfulness with another – (other than their other) – bears witness to the magnitude of hurt and angry feelings that arise to "justify" one's own response to be the same as the other's act – That they say "drove" them to this point! – [The word "choose" would not apply (in their mind at least) because they then would have to own the action that followed their reaction.]

Note: To share with you thoughts I had about Loyalty as Faithfulness being the foundation of one's committed primary relationship, I turn to my book Two – *Seeing Ourselves As Others See Us* (Our Personality Develops Through Person Perception And Self Experience):

Loyalty has become an archaic concept. Fidelity has been turned on its head becoming for many a sign of weakness. How does it start – This unfaithful process? We say "innocently enough" – (An interesting, but revealing choice of words). Our "innocence" begins with thoughts, is carried forth by feelings, and often culminates with acts. If our desire – (Especially we who have already lost our "innocence") is not to repeat ourselves, or if we are one of those who wonders what betrayal would be like – Hear me! – The process of unfaithfulness begins with a perception of whoever, thoughts, tempting thoughts follow, physiological "feelings" (more like "sensations") begin to stir and potentially unforgivable and unforgettable acts can follow.

The process of infidelity must be "nipped early in the bud" – It must not be given a chance to grow – I.e. if loyalty is part of our <u>becoming</u> the <u>way</u> we <u>want to be</u>. When thoughts of this "New Other" pop into our mind – (As they may, since we're only human) – We must immediately <u>replace</u> them. Hard perhaps to do but completely necessary – <u>Fantasies surrender to Memories</u> – (Memories of our other, <u>Sweet</u> memories, <u>Loving</u> memories). We think – We belong where our other is – We <u>belong with</u> our other – We <u>belong to</u> our other – Belonging to our other is a <u>choice not a have to</u> – <u>Choosing to belong</u> to our other far outweighs the chance we might take – Frankly, there is <u>no comparison</u>!

Therefore – To say <u>disloyalty begets disloyalty</u> is not to say that either party gets a "<u>free pass</u>"! –To say <u>anything otherwise</u> is to <u>deny</u> the <u>awful</u> and <u>traumatic impact</u> such a <u>betrayal reaps</u> on the <u>heart</u> and <u>soul</u> of the <u>betrayer and betrayed</u>.

No! "<u>Doubling down</u>" on this <u>particular kind</u> of <u>breach</u> of <u>loyalty</u> and <u>faithfulness</u> <u>cannot be mollified</u> <u>no matter what defenses</u> the <u>two offenders might choose</u> – I.e. – The <u>other's</u> disloyalty <u>came first</u>

(Projection). The other's disloyalty <u>made their other be disloyal</u> (Projection and Rationalization). [It doesn't matter <u>who went first</u> – <u>Both</u> in this primary relationship <u>made choices</u>. The <u>responsibilities</u> and <u>fallouts</u> of <u>both their choices</u> are <u>theirs</u> to <u>bear plus</u> the <u>consequences of what most surely will follow after</u>.] – It's <u>not taking away</u> from our primary relationship – If anything <u>it's enhancing it</u>! – [Oh yeah?!] [Be <u>introspectively honest</u> and <u>extrospectively honest</u> – "If it walks like a duck – it's a duck."]

The other thing to say about all of this is – Looking <u>inside and outside</u> ourselves at ourselves and then our other – How assertive have we been – (if these have been our needs) in letting our other know (by <u>speaking</u> to them <u>directly</u>, <u>openly</u>, and <u>honestly</u>) – What we would like from them – If they're willing and able to give them to us. – Hopefully, our other will assert back to us what they are willing and able to give us.

Questions:

- Can Loyalty become a <u>self righteous quality</u>? – [Indeed if we become full of ourselves and present ourselves accordingly] – And when we expect the other to be looking out for our best interests – when they clash with their best interests – Are we being unrealistic, naïve, stupid? – [Perhaps all three might apply. – But it's usually validated for us retrospectively – after the fact.]

- Take nothing for granted – How does this relate to loyalty? – [Validate, verify, be perceptive, assess, look for signs and then follow through.]

- Is Loyalty more essential to a relationship than Love? – [Very difficult to say.]

- Can we visualize a situation in which Loyalty to the other might be set aside? – [Yes – when the other proves to be disloyal – But is this ok or not?]

- When does Loyalty become a futile exercise? – Does it ever? – [Realizing the reality of it being only one way – When that sinks in – to the one needing to be loyal – that they're getting nothing back.]

- When might Loyalty be deemed manipulative? – [When it's <u>one way</u> – <u>We're giving</u> – the <u>other taking</u>.]

- Can we be loyal for both of us? – [No – But even if we could – What would be accomplished? – Loyalty would be <u>one-sided</u>.]

[A word or two before we move on about how one may tend to <u>rationalize their moves</u> if their interests are in another – (An other other than their other) – If they be "splitting hairs" when thinking about starting up or going ahead with a relationship outside their primary relationship. – [The caveat is that we must <u>own</u> our thoughts and feelings <u>first</u> – Then decide <u>what to do</u> about them – (<u>Before</u> we act – That is).]

Sometimes one's reasoning goes like this – Another relationship is ok so long as it's <u>not sexual</u>…

✓ just friends

✓ just someone to talk to

✓ just someone who listens

✓ just someone who understands

And as a result of our reciprocally asserting and validating we will come to realize – (If we hadn't already) – That most of what we need from our primary relationship – We <u>already have</u> in the <u>person we love</u> and <u>are loyal to</u>.

Question: Does loyalty have to be reciprocal in one's primary relationship to survive? – [Over time I think so]

- Is one-sided loyalty a healthy thing? – [See very little that's psychologically healthy about it.]
- Under what circumstances is one-sided loyalty an unhealthy thing? – [When it's one-sided.]

If you had to choose between Loyalty or Love from your other, which would you choose? – Love without Loyalty – Loyalty without Love – Which would you choose? – [Good question – How would you answer – Or have you answered it already? – If you have already chosen – (What does <u>had to</u> mean?)]

Question: Do we have the <u>right to assume</u> Loyalty from the other? – [There's always some <u>risk in assuming anything</u> when we think about it – But we do have the <u>right to validate what we're assuming</u>]

How do we validate Loyalty on the other's part? [By person perception – I.e. <u>perceiving what they present</u> – And most especially by <u>perceiving</u> their <u>acts that follow</u>.]

Can you conceptualize a relationship of <u>Loyalty without Love</u>? * What might be the motivating factor <u>for remaining</u> Loyal even when there is **<u>no longer</u> any Love? – [*Yes if there were <u>no Love</u> in the <u>first place</u>, **No longer any Love" implies that there <u>was once</u> Love there – Hope that if "<u>once there</u>" – it <u>might return</u>? – Hope Springs Eternal]

Are <u>narcissistic</u> people capable of Loyalty? – [Don't think so – Unhealthy Self Love – Preoccupation with Self – Full of Self – Can't get out of Self.]

<u>Can</u> there be <u>Love without Loyalty</u>? – [Hard to imagine – <u>Love</u> is <u>expressed through acts</u> of <u>Loyalty</u> – <u>Otherwise</u> it's <u>all talking</u> and <u>feeling</u>, but <u>no action</u>.]

71

Question: What would <u>motivate one</u> to <u>remain</u> <u>Loyal</u> to the <u>other who is not</u>?:

<u>From whence</u> does our need to remain Loyal – (Even when our other isn't) – <u>derive</u>?

<u>Negative Sources:</u>

- <u>Pity:</u> The <u>most dastardly</u> of motives for both the pityer and the pityee. To think that such a perception would even come to mind regarding the status and person of our other is <u>reprehensible</u>. Nor would our other – If they knew as much – Want to be perceived as such – (The <u>one</u> <u>exception</u> being one who might suffer from a <u>martyr complex</u>).
- <u>Guilt</u>: For what we may have done <u>unbeknownst</u> to other – So we reason – Who are <u>we to judge</u>? And so we <u>press</u> <u>on</u> (<u>guilty staying</u>, <u>guilty leaving</u>).
- <u>Loneliness</u>: <u>Having someone around</u> is <u>better</u> than <u>no one</u>.

- <u>Long Suffering</u>: It's in our <u>make-up</u> – For us especially if we see this as our "<u>lot in life</u>" and thus "<u>get off</u>" at <u>pitying self</u>.

- <u>Poor Self Concept</u>: <u>Introspectively</u> we conclude the other is <u>all that we deserve</u>.

- <u>Low Self Esteem</u>: We're <u>lucky</u> to have what we do.

- <u>Attachment Disorder</u>: <u>Hold on for dear life</u>. What better way to describe one's <u>desperation</u>!

- <u>Make Up For One's Own Disloyalty</u>: Back to <u>guilt</u> being the <u>chief motivator</u> – Especially if one perceives one's <u>own disloyalty</u> to be <u>greater than</u> the <u>other's</u>.

- <u>Last But Not Least</u>: The <u>one trait</u> – (I.e. To Be Loyal) the other <u>values above all</u> (even though <u>they</u> themselves <u>have come up short</u>). – We <u>use it</u> in order to "<u>hold on</u>" to the other.

Positive Sources: – [Note – We call these positive even though over time they may <u>turn</u> out to be <u>not so positive</u> for us.]

- Love: We <u>love</u> the <u>other</u> even though the <u>other</u> is <u>not loyal</u> – Is love enough without loyalty – Especially if it's <u>missing</u> from the other? – What does "<u>enough</u>" mean? – <u>Psychologically</u> speaking? <u>Theologically</u> speaking? <u>Both</u>?

- Devotion: Significantly it relates to an <u>aspect of worship</u>. For some it's not too much a stretch to say that "one worships the ground the other walks on."
  [Note that for some of these positives in the long run they can <u>turn out negative</u> especially if <u>they affect one's perception</u> of what is <u>really happening</u>.]

- Religion: <u>Our religion says so</u> – We're "<u>all in</u>" with our Loyalty – The <u>exception if</u> the other is <u>disloyal</u> in <u>one particular way</u> – I.e. <u>Unfaithful Sexually With Another</u> – If the other is <u>disloyal</u> in <u>any other way</u>, <u>what then</u>? – [We'll be discussing this at length when we ask the question – If Loyalty is one of your – (If not the <u>most</u> <u>important</u>) needs you have in your personality – What does this make you susceptible to in your relationship with an other?]

Question: If your need to be a loyal person is large what potentially hurt/harm might befall you?

"It is better to have loved and lost than never to have loved at all" – [Note: That this doesn't address whether the other loved you in the process.]

Likewise – Can we substitute Loyalty for Love and would this still be psychologically true? – [In both cases (Love and Loyalty) – The "better" part depends upon the realization that we were doing the loving and being loyal – And that is a very psychologically good thing that validates who we are and what we're capable of.]

Switching gears now we're going to be addressing what is meant when one makes the commitment to be loyal to our other while "forsaking all others."

"Forsaking All Others" – What does this mean? Who "Exactly Others" are we talking about? "Forsaking" is a pretty powerful word – Taken literally it could mean removing ourselves from others, having nothing to do with others anymore, cutting ourselves off from any further involvement.

Surely, this is taking it – (Forsaking) – Too far – Or isn't it? – Some have interpreted it this way – And this has allowed them to rationalize the neglect (or in some cases) abandonment of others – (once or still) important to them – [Why do children and parents come immediately to mind!]

- ✓ Putting our other before our parents?
- ✓ Putting our other before their parents?
- ✓ Putting ourselves before our parents?
- ✓ Putting ourselves before their parents?

What's going on? Is this what we (and our other) promised to do?

We can hardly believe that we vowed to do this!

Surely it goes without saying that we won't take it to this degree! [Oh yeah? Let's take a "look see".] …

Why does one's or the other's <u>mother-in-law</u> (<u>or father-in-law</u>) come to mind? Lest we forget, we're talking about our mother and/or father and our other's mother and/or father as well.

Typically, it's the contention that <u>mothers-in-law</u> can be <u>more</u> a challenge <u>than fathers-in-law</u> in this <u>connection</u>.

And "Connection" it is – A special connection between "children" and parents that won't go away even for a day. Clearly, "forsaking all others" did not mean cutting off or even interrupting this connection – [Let's face it, that's not likely to happen.] But we're not talking about a <u>continuation</u> of the <u>same connection</u> – (I.e. the <u>same level</u> of connection (<u>as before</u>)) – We're talking about the connection "<u>stepping up</u> a notch or two" – [Why does "<u>momma's boy</u>" or "<u>daddy's girl</u>" now come to mind?]

If the <u>connections</u> of our <u>past</u>, and <u>present</u>, <u>continue</u> into the future of our primary relationship and seem to <u>loom even larger</u> what can become of this?

What can become of this? – To begin with, <u>conflictions</u> over the <u>connections</u> – Little by little having to choose between loyalties. Contests, debates, cost vs reward discussions (provided there are discussions at all) about who should come first, on whom shall we spend our time and energy – (And this is the Big One – Who needs us the most? – (Or maybe one should be reflecting upon the question that's tugging at us – Whom do we need the most?)

Torn loyalties lead more to confrontation than discussion. Movements toward one and away from the other are closely scrutinized and criticized. Frustrations mount. Tempers flare. What words are said and how they're said combine to give each other the perception that "forsaking all others" does not apply in this exception. The unintended result of which – All parties are offended – Rivalries are tested – There are no winners.

What's the resolution? – (If there is such in this connection) – [We're in a "gray area" here pertains] – Sharing ourselves and our other with our respective others – (in this case – parents). Each in our primary relationship being willing to assert and listen to our other regarding how much.

Do these conflicts of loyalties negatively affect the reciprocal loyalty we look for and subsequently positively experience otherwise in our primary relationship? – [You bet they do. Somebody's going to be "short-changed" – And it's usually one or the other or (for that matter) both in our primary relationship.]

This is an example of presenting an example of what may happen (and often does) without having any answer for what to do if and when it does. Then it's an example of – without an answer for.

How all of this plays out – (If it hasn't already – (Now or maybe in the future)) – depends to a great extent on the respective personalities of the two who have come together in a reciprocally loving and loyal primary relationship.

Each is willing to give of ourselves and our other to those outside our primary relationship to those who need us or to those we need – (For example our respective parents).

The mandate that our other should come first can be reciprocally realistically modified by existing circumstances – So that those most important others

within our circle of love will have their share of us –
But <u>not at the expense of our other</u>!

The same holds true for the <u>children</u> (<u>not our own</u>) who may come into our life because of our other. Certainly out of <u>deference</u> to our other and our other to us we will <u>not allow whatever adjustments</u> we have to make <u>jeopardize</u> the <u>love</u> and <u>loyalty</u> we have <u>pledged</u> to <u>each other</u>.

An answer to why there's this "<u>push</u> and <u>pull</u>" <u>going</u> on in our <u>respective lives</u> may lie in <u>how our respective personalities have developed</u> through person perception and self experience in our <u>respective families</u> of <u>origin</u>. Co-dependent caretakers – in control experiences with parents and attachments that accordingly <u>occur</u> and <u>extend</u> throughout our "<u>adult-child-life</u>." Sometimes in a <u>parallel</u> way, other times "<u>intersecting</u>" with or <u>interjecting</u> into our "<u>grown-up-child-life</u>" and <u>indirectly</u> or <u>directly</u> into our primary relationship life – a life we <u>entered</u> into and <u>promised</u> would <u>always come first</u>.

Especially when personalities clash within and outside our primary relationship, <u>choices</u> we deem important will have to be made. <u>Hard</u> choices. Avoidance – Avoidance Choices. We two, in our primary relationship, find ourselves between a "rock and a hard place" and our allegiance to whom? – Intermittently visited. Sharing our other's love and loyalty with others – Be they our other's parents or children – We can <u>accept albeit sometimes grudgingly</u> – (Especially if or when this sharing takes away our other's time and energy from sharing themselves with our parents or the children we share together. There's <u>only so much time</u> and <u>energy</u> that we have to give each other when <u>others</u> very important to us to be sure are <u>tapping into</u> the <u>limited supply</u> that we have to offer. In any case it behooves us to <u>make sure</u> we <u>have more than enough left over for each other</u>.

While we're on the subject of there being not enough time and energy to go around – That means above all we have to <u>learn how to prioritize</u> the same that we don't have enough of. We've been talking how what's going on with our children, our respective parents can leave us with very little time and energy for each other. Well – Speaking of something that uses up even more of our time and energy – (and this

probably is putting it mildly) – is our work life –
[whether we both work outside the home or one or the
other of us works at home] – We would probably
agree that at the end of the day – We have little time
or energy to focus on each other.

While we're on the subject of work – Especially
looking at what life is like for us in our workplace – and
considering how things are going for us especially with
respect to loyalty in our workplace – What happens to
us in our workplace (would we not agree) impacts us
big-time both in our workplace and at home in our
primary relationship. Again to repeat what happens at
our workplace especially with respect to how we are
treated – [I.e. How we perceive they perceive us and
how we perceive ourselves!] can and often does
adversely affect our health and happiness in our
primary relation when reciprocal loyalty is not present
and exercised in our workplace.

Consider the following relationships that play out
in our workplace:

Employer→Employee

Employee→Employer

Employer←→Employee (reciprocal loyalty)

Questions:

- Can there be Loyalty amongst <u>unequals</u>? [Maybe what we're looking for doesn't exist – I.e. cannot exist!]
- Is our workplace an example of Loyalty in a <u>controlled</u> setting? [Could be – Probably is.]
- Is Reciprocal Loyalty in our workplace <u>realistically possible</u>? [How would one characterize the dynamic of such?...<u>Mutual respect</u> for each other <u>despite</u> the <u>differences</u> in <u>position</u> and <u>status</u>.]
- If someone is <u>first</u> and <u>foremost loyal</u> to an <u>entity</u> such as a company <u>should we expect</u> any <u>Loyalty to come our way</u>? [What do we think.]
- How does "<u>Bottom Line" thinking and perceiving</u> relate to Loyalty? ["Bottom Line" one-ups Loyalty!]

- Can Loyalty exist in an atmosphere where <u>everyone</u> is <u>expendable</u>? – Everyone from the top on down? – [Does this <u>neutralize inequality</u>?]

- No hard feelings! – It's just business! – We're sure you understand – [Sure we do!!]

- How does the phrase – What have you <u>done for me lately</u> relate to loyalty? [Loyal is as Loyal does – So keep on doing (until we drop?!)]

- You are <u>no longer useful</u> to me! You've <u>outlived</u> your usefulness. It's <u>costing us too much</u> to keep you. <u>Your time has passed</u> you. Your Loyalty <u>doesn't count</u> for anything.

- We <u>don't owe</u> you anything <u>for what you've done</u> for us in the past – That was <u>then</u> – This is <u>now</u>!

- You have become <u>a liability</u> for us.

- We're <u>not going to fire</u> you <u>because</u> then <u>you</u> can <u>collect unemployment</u> – [How low can one go!!]

No – We're going to insidiously – behind the scenes – make your work life as <u>difficult</u> and <u>unpleasant</u> and <u>unrewarding</u> as we can – So that sooner rather than later <u>you'll</u> finally <u>get fed up</u> with the whole situation and <u>quit</u>. And on top of all this we can <u>rationalize away any part</u> that <u>we</u> might have <u>played</u> in <u>your demise and wash</u> our <u>hands of any particle of guilt we</u> may have <u>felt</u>. "It was a <u>business decision</u>." How this resonates with the <u>collateral fallout</u> within the workplace. "Commitment" (if we can call it that) – The "<u>commitment</u>" <u>only so far</u> as the <u>contract</u> goes – If <u>no contract</u> – Guess what – We <u>don't need</u> a <u>reason</u> [Where have we heard this before?]

Sounds like we've been there, done that. So much for loyalty in the workplace! The <u>impact</u> on one's life is <u>inestimable</u>. For many <u>workplace</u> is our "<u>second home</u>" <u>trumped only by our home</u> and <u>family</u>, and <u>all</u> we <u>get from</u> our <u>workplace</u> is "<u>loyalty be damned!</u>"

The Litmus Test For Loyalty

Time to get up close and personal. It's time for us to ask ourselves what we look for in determining <u>whether or not our loved one is loyal</u>. What's the saying? Loyal <u>is</u> what Loyal <u>does</u>!

What is our <u>Litmus Test</u> – That we can see how we're doing before we proceed to measure our other? – <u>Introspectively</u> do we have <u>in our personality</u> the <u>attributes</u> that <u>make</u> up <u>Loyalty</u>? <u>First</u> of all we must <u>know what to look for</u>. <u>Secondly</u>, we must <u>lower</u> our <u>defenses</u> because these tend to <u>distort</u> our <u>perceptions</u> so that we <u>end up seeing what we want to see rather than what is really there</u>. What we would <u>like</u> to <u>see</u> is a <u>loyal person</u> who <u>has</u> the <u>qualities</u> in their <u>personality</u> that we then could <u>present</u> as a <u>loyal person</u>. <u>Presenting</u> as a <u>loyal person</u> for our <u>other to perceive</u> – (having <u>lowered</u> our <u>defenses</u> – so that we can <u>now trust</u> our <u>perceptions</u>) – We are able to directly, <u>openly</u> and <u>honestly demonstrate</u> – in <u>words</u> and <u>acts</u> – <u>that we are a loyal person</u>.

We present to our other in words and acts that…

- ✓ They can trust us
- ✓ That we take responsibility for our thoughts, feelings and actions
- ✓ That our other can depend on us
- ✓ That promises made will be promises kept
- ✓ That they can count on us because we're accountable
- ✓ Last – but surely not least – that we will be faithful – because we believe in our selves – that we can be faithful to our other

We would hope <u>our other has likewise taken the litmus test for loyalty</u> (having lowered their defenses so <u>they too</u> can <u>trust</u> their <u>perceptions</u>) and in the process <u>found</u> these <u>attributes</u> in <u>their personality</u> that they will <u>present</u> to <u>us</u> <u>directly</u>, <u>openly</u> and <u>honestly</u> and that <u>believing in themselves</u> and <u>us</u>, they can then <u>be faithful</u> to <u>themselves</u> and <u>us</u>. The <u>result</u> of such <u>reciprocal introspection</u> will be <u>reciprocal loyalty</u> and <u>faithfulness</u>. [We wish this for us all.]

We <u>both pass</u> the <u>litmus test</u> of <u>loyalty</u>. But keeping in mind that no two people are exactly alike. <u>One</u> may <u>turn out</u> to be <u>better at</u> this <u>loyalty thing</u> than the <u>other</u>. That's probably because no two personalities are exactly alike. And that's because <u>our personalities developed through our own person perception and self experience</u> – That is, <u>what we were exposed to</u> – <u>What</u> we <u>perceived</u> – And <u>how</u> we <u>interpreted</u> what we perceived – And <u>how</u> we <u>ended up feeling</u> about our Selves when we perceived our Selves. All these perceptions gave us a picture of ourselves – and <u>how</u> we felt – when we looked at our picture – became our <u>self worth</u>.

All of this is to say that if the two of us are loyal to begin with – It goes without saying that we <u>committed</u> to each other – that we intended <u>to stay that way</u> (so help us God). Remember that what we have said about <u>one-sided loyalty</u> – It's a very <u>unhealthy</u> thing – If <u>that's all there is</u> to perpetuate and sustain our primary relationship. Some of us believe that <u>love can compensate for what loyalty may be missing</u>. That's of course <u>assuming</u> that <u>love</u> is <u>two-way</u>. It's hard to imagine that the <u>one not loyal</u> to the other can still claim to love the other. Remember we have said the acts of love are acts of loyalty. Sometimes we like to think we have enough love in us for two and enough loyalty in us for two. Even if this were true – unreciprocated love and loyalty can abide but surely not go on to last.

So what then? Those who have narrowly defined love and loyalty for and from their other to mean as long as our other hasn't taken up with another (and this usually means sexually) loyalty and love can still exist. Absent manifestation of such occurrence, the loyal one tells themselves that all is well – defensively in denial about all the other qualities of reciprocal love and loyalty that might be missing.

If our need to be loyal is greater than our need for the other to be loyal we are opening ourselves up to expect more from ourselves than our other. In some instances we may be perceiving loyalty in our other that isn't there. If this may be true – We need to start perceiving our other as they really are – and not as We wish them to be. [This is one of our defenses to project upon our other qualities that really aren't there

– Thus making our other look better and making ourselves feel better about what we see.]

This is why it's so important that we validate. If we know what we're looking for – but we can't see inside our other – And if it is there – but our other is not presenting it for us to see – Validating loyalty's qualities within our other becomes very difficult.

The trouble is that when our defenses are high – We have great difficulty perceiving the reality of what's before us. We distort perceptual cues that our other may be unknowingly presenting. Or it may be that our other is presenting only what our other knows we want to see – (no more, no less) – If only unfaithfulness perpetrated with an other can be seen by us and be judged by us as the one and only commitment breaker – Absent this kind of unforgivable betrayal, especially if we thought and felt at commitment time that our other thought and felt the same – I.e. that faithfulness of this sort was reciprocally a "given." If faithfulness is reciprocally a "given" then what else is left to worry about or even be concerned about as we live out our lives together, having pledged a life of reciprocal love, loyalty and faithfulness. There is the caveat pertaining to those of us who <u>may be</u> or <u>become satisfied</u> with the <u>status quo</u> of our primary relationship – So long as this <u>one act</u> of <u>unfaithfulness</u> is not <u>perpetrated</u> by <u>us</u> upon our <u>other</u>, nor by our <u>other upon us</u>. What we're trying to get to is this! If we are looking for faithfulness in ourselves for our other and faithfulness in our other for us – We need to <u>look further</u> than we are used to doing – to <u>see what else</u> might be <u>included</u> in our <u>quest</u> for <u>faithfulness</u>!

<u>Narrowly defining disloyalty</u> and <u>unfaithfulness</u> – as we are wont to do – can result in <u>neglecting</u> to look at the <u>larger picture</u> – We need to <u>hone in</u> on what <u>we</u> may <u>have been missing because we weren't looking for it in</u> the <u>right places</u> and <u>therefore didn't realize</u> that what we <u>were looking for in ourselves</u> and <u>our other</u> – (If the truth be told) – wasn't there.

What we're going to be looking for now as together we peruse the <u>whole picture</u> is <u>what each of us</u> might be <u>susceptible to</u> when <u>perpetrated</u> by <u>ourselves</u> or our <u>other</u> – which may lead us to have a very different perception of ourselves and our other. The "Big One" in this <u>instance</u> is one <u>we don't</u> even <u>want to think about</u> happening in our primary relationship i.e. that <u>we</u> or our <u>other</u> could <u>possibly</u> be an <u>abuser</u>, an <u>abusee</u> or <u>both</u>.

[The following are extractions from my third book: *The Gray Area of Psychological Abuse.* Subtitled: Abuser, Abusee, Or Both: How Can We Tell, What Can We Do?]

Physical and Sexual Abuse within our primary relationship we would hope would be obvious breaches of our commitment of reciprocal loyalty and faithfulness. <u>Other behaviors</u> indicative of <u>psychological abuse</u> if present seem not to draw as much attention. One plausible reason for this may be that they are so <u>commonplace</u> in our everyday lives that we hardly give ourselves cause to notice them.

Once again it may be <u>our defenses</u> are <u>working overtime</u> to the end that we pay not much mind to what is happening to us – and (in the long run) – hurting us. Each of us, therefore is asked to <u>look closely at ourselves, at our other, at our primary relationship</u> and see <u>introspectively</u> as well as <u>extrospectively</u> what (<u>if anything</u>) <u>is happening</u> that we may be <u>doing</u> to our <u>other</u> – Or our <u>other</u> may be doing to us – that qualifies as a <u>sampling</u> of <u>verbal and/or non-verbal psychological abuse</u> – (and as such – could constitute a <u>breach</u> of <u>love, loyalty and faithfulness</u>).

We need to be <u>honestly subjective</u> and <u>objective</u> in following through with this. Above all – We will need once more to <u>lower</u> our <u>defenses</u> – so that then we will be able to <u>trust</u> our <u>perceptions</u>. Remember only then can we have confidence that we are <u>seeing ourselves as we really are</u> and <u>determine how this matches up with how we want to be</u>. Would that our <u>other</u> will <u>do</u> the <u>same</u>. So that reciprocally we can <u>see how well</u> or <u>how poorly we may be treating one another</u> in our primary relationship.

Looking at our primary relationship validating how we're doing – (No matter how hard we find this to do) – It all will be worth it – So long as both we and our other are willing to <u>own</u> what we've been <u>doing</u> (and <u>how</u> we've been <u>acting</u>) – that has <u>come</u> up <u>short</u> – and are <u>willing</u> to <u>do what we can</u> to <u>change what needs changing</u>.

One last thing – before we identify forms of psychological abuse – and that is – <u>Don't Give Up!</u> Looking at these and thinking they don't apply because it's strictly a "<u>gender thing.</u>" <u>It isn't.</u> <u>Both sexes</u> can <u>behave like this</u> and <u>act like this</u>. It's a <u>human thing</u>! ["We're only human."]

[From book three - ...*The Gray Area of Psychological Abuse*...]

Hypercritical – Let's say the other (keep in mind that there's always the possibility that we could be the other – only our defenses to date won't let us see that) – [Incidentally, this will hold true for all the other forms of psychological abuse as well.] – Let's say the other is constantly criticizing what we say or do – especially after the fact.

Either we have let them know what we said or did – (because, after all, they are the other in our primary relationship – and we want to be able to share with them – what's going on in our life) – Or someone else tells them – Or some other way they find out.

In any case – our wish is for them to listen and positively respond – Instead we get the should-haves and the why-didn't-yous – The how-comes – The I would-haves – And we end up either having to defend ourselves – Or having to say "yes Dear" – "You're right Dear" – (And not mean a word of it – But just to get them off our back).

What is likely to happen – if this scenario keeps repeating itself – is that the one who is constantly being criticized by the other – after the fact – will seriously curtail – if not stop altogether – sharing information about their activities with their other.

This in itself will change the dynamics of the interaction between the two – But not in a healthy, positive way. Because there are other ways already mentioned that the other can find out what's been going on – Including asking the other point blank – (I.e. the other who's no longer volunteering the information) – The other not wanting to lie – speaks up – and the cycle of criticism of the other – by the other continues.

Nagging – can become abusive to the psyche. Operationally defined – nagging involves – keeping after a person with one's words and tone in an increasingly irritating and annoying way – (Which characterizes how it is experienced by both the nagger and the naggee).

The naggee finds it particularly annoying and irritating when it's a case of the nagger beating the naggee to the punch – I.e. the naggee was just about to start a project – Had it presently in their mind – And along comes the command <u>neutralizing the initiative</u> – and making it feel every bit a <u>have-to</u> rather than a <u>choose-to</u>. The "it's about time you" – Puts the finishing touches on <u>ruining anything positive</u> one might gain from the experience.

The nagger in this case feels justified in keeping after the other – Because if they don't – nothing will get done. If anyone is being abused by the other – the nagger feels they are – By the lack of cooperation – the procrastination – the putting other things first – the ignoring of their wishes.

Could we have here a case of both parties feeling abused by the other? – We could have and we probably do have. Abuser? Abusee? Both? – In this case, both!

Hitting The Other Below The Belt…is another form of psychologically abusive behavior. Say – The other shared something about themselves from their past – very private and very personal – They haven't told anyone else about it – because it was too embarrassing for them to talk about – Plus, they were still struggling to deal with it – They took a big risk laying bare their soul to us.

And how do we respond to their trust – (Or the other to us – If it's the other way around) – In a moment of frustration and anger – Or when we might be hurting and want to hurt back – We bring up the issue and in a hurtful, mean-spirited way – Throw it in their face – and Rub their nose in it. Worst of all – In one fell swoop – We betray their trust. How could we? – Or if it's the other way around – How could they!

<u>Bringing behavioral samples from our mutual past</u> – of how they let us down – Didn't come through for us – Didn't do what they said they would – Didn't

give us what they promised us – This is a particularly insidious psychologically abusive tool that the other (Or we if we're the abuser) turns to – when they're out of ammunition relating to the present. It's particularly insidious – because we can't get a handle on it – It seems to be thrown in there – to get us off track. The point is – Neither We – (Nor our Other – for that matter) – can <u>prove</u> – one way – or the other – the <u>veracity</u> of <u>their allegations</u>.

Even if some of their allegations were true – We can't <u>undo</u> what <u>has been said</u> or <u>done</u>. The <u>context</u> of the <u>past is no more</u>. There is <u>nothing we can do or say in our defense</u>. <u>Intellectually</u> we know this – But <u>emotionally</u> – we feel unjustly put upon – We say to ourselves this is "Dirty Pool" – But so saying to ourselves – doesn't ameliorate the feeling – that we have been psychologically abused.

Belittling – "Be little" – That's the intent of the belittler – That we be little – smaller – after they're through with us – They want with their tone and words – (usually sarcastic and biting) – to cut us off at the knees. Their overall desire is that the <u>picture</u> we have of ourselves – and the way we <u>feel</u> about that picture be <u>diminished greatly</u>.

The belittler uses their <u>cognitive verbal</u> side to attack our <u>mental side</u>. The abuser employs the nimbleness of their mind – The quickness of their wit – The cleverness of their words to talk down to us – By talking above us – Giving us the perception of their perception of us – That we don't know much – That we're intellectually inferior – Or – at our best – Know far less than they do.

A variation of belittling are the "<u>mind games</u>" two potential abusers "play." The intellectual jousting – The cognitive – incisive – caustic exchange that starts out "innocently enough" – But quickly accelerates into a competitive fervor – Tempers flare – Words get nastier – There is no winner – Minds exhausted – Emotions worse for wear.

Herein the psychological abuse <u>is at least reciprocal</u>. Two minds duking it out. Probably the best that can be said is that it <u>at least wasn't one-sided and let it go at that</u>!

Berating – Treating our other like they had dropped several notches in our favorable rating system – (from B rate to D or even F rate)

The abusee metaphorically is like a stake in the ground with notches on it – that we're systematically pounding into the ground – Whatever point we are trying to drive home – Whatever they did or said we didn't like – Whatever they didn't do that we counted on – We keep belaboring the point ad nauseam until our other pleads – No More! – Or we have exhausted ourselves.

The end result of the incessant pounding is that the abusee feels beaten up psychologically and the abuser feels physically tired. Two distinctive outcomes that help distinguish abuser from abusee – When we think about it.

Trifling With The Other's Emotions – This form of psychological abuse involves one trivializing something or someone very important to the other – that or who – the other takes very seriously.

In this case the abuser's MO may be to mock – Or make fun of – Or tell jokes about someone the other looks up to – or something the other values – or has a strong belief in. Typically the <u>abusee</u> views such <u>bad behavior</u> – as the <u>abuser</u> being <u>disrespectful</u> – <u>intolerant</u> – <u>insensitive</u> – <u>uncaring</u> of the <u>abusee's feelings, opinions or beliefs</u>.

<u>A Word About Joking</u> – About things the other is relatively serious about – Jokes made in the context of our relationship often have a <u>double meaning</u>.

The joker may say that they were just kidding – (Especially if the joke backfires) – But more often than not – The joker is trying to say something – They are being very indirect about – That if they were direct about – The other <u>would not appreciate</u> much and <u>probably get upset</u> and <u>angry</u>.

<u>Taking The Other For Granted</u> – or if we're the abusee, <u>being taken for granted</u>. The dynamic involved is – There's no showing of appreciation for

what we do – for the other – nor what the other has done for us.

No thank you's – No compliments – No acknowledgements of their value to us. Certainly, no special recognition. All of this is a <u>gross failure to appreciate</u> and could be rightly referred to as a <u>psychological abuse stemming from omission</u>.

Treating The Other Like They're Our Built-In, Home Grown Bound Servant – <u>Ordering</u> them around in <u>military fashion</u>. Giving the impression that they're there to <u>do our bidding</u> – Implying by our attitude, words and actions that <u>their life belongs to us</u> – That <u>they don't have one of their own</u>.

Embarrassing Or Humiliating The Other In Front Of Others – <u>Going public</u> with something that was <u>supposed</u> to be <u>private</u>. Sharing a deficiency of the other's with others. Acting toward the other in such a way that it spells out for all to see – For none to miss – That we <u>are in charge of "you know who!"</u> In general, behaving poorly so the other ends up <u>embarrassed to be with us</u>. All of these behaviors are indicative of psychological abuse.

<u>Failing to Psychologically Support The Other In "Crunch Time"</u> – Giving the other the impression that we're <u>one hundred percent behind them</u> – That we <u>feel like they do</u> about something they feel strongly about – But, When it's time for us to <u>take</u> a <u>stand</u> and <u>speak</u> our <u>mind</u> and <u>back</u> our other – We <u>wilt</u> under the pressure and <u>wimp</u> out – More concerned about how <u>we look</u> to others than we are about what <u>our other</u> must be <u>going through</u> – Now standing alone! This is called "Hanging The Other Out To Dry" – <u>Saving our own skin at their expense</u>.

Sometimes it involves "Switching Sides" in the middle of the contest – Letting the other swim upstream on their own – Other times it may mean One-Upping them – Showing them up in front of others.

To reiterate what the Purpose was – To ask us to perceive ourselves and our other with regard to whether we – or our other – or both of us – may be abusees or abusers or both – When relating to each other in our one and only committed primary relationship – The <u>Purpose</u> being that <u>we not fixate upon sexual activity of either of us with an other outside our primary relation – And in so doing conclude that such behavior be the one and only "bond breaker" when addressing the state of our reciprocally committed Love, Loyal and Faithful relationship</u>.

The <u>risk</u> of being <u>fixated</u> on only <u>one aspect</u> of Love, Loyalty and Faithfulness – (Even if we deem it most important) – Is that we look no further to perceive – assert – and validate – how we and our other are doing in our committed primary relationship.

What we need to do then – Using person perception and Self experience – as the tools for our Self and Other's examination – is for each of us to perceive ourselves – To perceive our other – And to perceive our other perceiving us – with regard to how each of us is <u>presenting ourselves reciprocally to the other</u>.

Using the operationally defined forms of psychological abuse as a subjective and objective Measuring Stick – How do We fare – How does our other fare?...

When we looked at the examples of how others psychologically abuse each other – Were we drawn as a magnet to any of them – To all of them? – If so, What was our reaction? Did we say to ourselves – That's Me! – Or, That's my Other! – Or, That's how my other looks at me! – We can't believe how "close to home" your words have come – It's hard to look at myself and my other like this!

This exercise of turning myself <u>in</u> – to look at myself – And turning myself <u>out</u> to look at my other – Is part and parcel of our quest for Love, Loyalty and Faithfulness – It addresses as perhaps never before how each of us is doing in keeping the Commitment we made to each other – I.e. to Love, Cherish, be Loyal and Faithful to each other.

But What If Our Other Doesn't Change?
What Then?

Remember what we said – "To Be Loyal" – was all about – We said "To Be Loyal" meant that we would be Trustworthy – Responsible – Dependable – Accountable and Truthful.

This means – to start with – We must lower our defenses – So that we then can trust our perceptions – And then having done this see whether we have these qualities – When we look at ourselves. If we do – Then we need to ask ourselves – Are we presenting these to our other? If we see some of them – But not all of them – Be not dismayed! – There is still hope for us. – Changes can be made – Not wholesale changes – But change enough to make things better for our Selves and our Other.

[In my Book Five – *Don't Like The Way It Is, Change It*] – We look in depth at what we <u>don't like</u> about ourselves – And what we don't like about our other. But, as we surely should, we also look at what we <u>do like</u> about ourselves and our other. And we assured ourselves that — (perhaps with help) — we could change our commitment to each other — From for "Better or for Worse" — To "Better and even Better."

The subtitle of Book Five is "Changing Before Or After An Ultimatum." This addresses the reality that even though a commitment is made — For "better or for worse" — Our primary relationship — When we look closely at it — May not be doing well — And may even be doing worse.

We've been telling ourselves — It's not so bad — That it could be worse. Maybe we're in denial — Maybe we're the "Eternal Optimist" — Maybe we're saying to ourselves — I can relate — I can adjust — There's too much at stake — Maybe <u>I</u> need to change <u>first</u> — And <u>not wait</u> — for my <u>Other</u> to change.

Maybe I need to find someone that I can talk to — To share my thoughts, feelings and needs with. Someone who can perceive — By my self report — What I'm perceiving — And thus perceive the reality that I'm perceiving — And thus be able to empathize with what I am dealing with.

[And so we go to someone for help – (Even as they've come to me for help these past thirty-five years) – <u>Support Therapy Clinic</u> is the name I gave it so many years ago because that's how I saw – (and still see) – What I am – And what I do – is all about – I.e. Helping People Help Themselves – And thus as a result have a Healthier and Happier Life that they deserve.]

Indeed, <u>changing begins with us</u> – We need to be given the insight about what We need to change and upon our self report what our Other needs to change.

Once we own what we need to change – And with support begin to change – Our presentation to our other will change – As we go forth with <u>new verbal</u> and <u>nonverbal behaviors</u> for our other to perceive.

But what about our Other? – Does our Other even notice changes we are making – Changes in our presentation with regard to a dramatic lessening of forms of psychological abuse we formerly were presenting – Supplanted – as it were – by words of

<u>caring</u> and <u>supporting</u> and <u>acts</u> of <u>empathy</u> and <u>listening</u>.

The other things we may be doing differently is <u>asserting</u> to our other what we need from them – Directly, Openly and Honestly – (Starting our sentences with "I") – And – <u>Validating</u> first with our other, what we think is going on with them – Before we rush to <u>perceptual judgments</u> – Which could very easily then become <u>value judgments</u>.

About our Other changing – What are the chances of that happening? – Our other would probably not know what they need to change – (Especially if they're in denial) – If they are not coming to the need for them to change – What Then?

When we assert to our other – <u>What we need from them</u> – We probably in some cases are asking pretty much for the <u>opposite</u> of <u>how</u> they are <u>presenting to us</u>.

If we begin by saying – You need to change this or that – They'll probably feel "attacked" – "Coming up short" – As it were – [That's why we need to start our presentation with "I".]

If what "I" need is what my other <u>can't</u> or <u>won't</u> give me – What Then? – [<u>I hope</u> – <u>I can "adjust" won't immediately</u> be part of the picture.]

You have already "adjusted" – (If you will) – By seeking help – And with that help supporting you – You're changing. Psychological abuse – in your case – I.e. with you being the one presenting it has been curtailed – Through your consistent, persistent awareness of the thoughts and feelings you had (in the <u>past</u>) – And may still have (in the <u>present</u>) – That priorly led to <u>psychologically abusive verbal</u> and <u>nonverbal acts</u> directed at your Other…So…

- So <u>you're</u> changing and becoming the kind of person you've decided you want to be.
- Perceiving your other over time – Instances of psychological abuse have continued – There's been <u>little</u> – if any – change on your other's part.
- You have <u>caringly confronted</u> your Other about what you're needing from your other – I.e. <u>what you're missing</u> that <u>only</u> your <u>other</u> can <u>provide</u>.

- You were <u>assertive enough</u> to ask your other – If they were <u>willing</u> to <u>seek</u> some <u>therapeutic help</u>. Your Other knows that's what <u>You did</u> and <u>still are doing</u>.

<u>Question</u>: Do we have the <u>right</u> to ask the other to change? – To <u>act differently</u> – To <u>talk differently</u> – To <u>treat</u> us <u>differently</u>? – [Of course we do.]

But what about the "beam in our own eye" – <u>Let the changing begin with us</u> – We <u>say</u> this – We must <u>mean</u> this – We must <u>do</u> this!

Surely there are things about ourselves we would <u>like to change</u>. Some we would like to make have to do with <u>our Relationship</u> – Some of them have to do just with <u>our Person</u> – Maybe, some of the changes we make will have the <u>desired effect</u> on the <u>other</u> – that we wish for – But if not – The changes will be <u>good for us</u> anyway – We'll be <u>stronger</u> and <u>feel better</u> about ourselves.

What characteristics of our other are <u>resistant</u> to change? Sometimes our other comes right out with it with <u>defenses blazing</u> – And says things we can't believe we're hearing.

What do you say to the person who says – [When you married me you knew how I was – You knew I wasn't going to change – So, what's up with "I gotta change stuff?" – Did you really think you could change me? – Who made you the arbiter of change? – Nothing you can say or do can/will make me change! – Change? – What's there to change? – I like the way I am!]

What's been <u>happening to you</u> in the <u>company of the other</u>? – This is critical for us to assess – Whether we look <u>better</u> or <u>worse</u> to <u>ourself</u> – When we're <u>with</u> our <u>other</u> – Whether we stay with – Or leave – our other – Can have more to do with <u>how we feel about ourselves</u> – When we're with our other – Than how we <u>feel about them</u> – When we're with our other.

What if We change but our <u>Other</u> doesn't? – Do we have to accept that this is the way it is – And going to be? – Or, do we have <u>alternatives</u>? – How do we <u>go about deciding</u> what to do?

Okay, the situation is this – We put it out there – How we <u>feel</u> – What we <u>need</u> – What we're <u>willing to</u>

<u>do</u> to change things – (Some of these changes we're <u>already making</u>).

What's the other doing? – Zippo – Nothing – Our other hasn't budged an inch – It's like talking to a stone wall – <u>Now what</u>!

But here's the thing that bothers Me most about our situation – I feel <u>I've</u> been doing my part to change – Whatever I need to change – To make our relationship better – I've been going to therapy – So I can better understand myself – And have a better understanding of what's happening to us.

Now it's Your turn – <u>I'm</u> trying to change and grow – But I don't see <u>You</u> doing any changing. It wasn't <u>easy</u> for me to make the decision to <u>get help</u>. My first thought was I should be able to do this <u>on my own</u>. Now I <u>know differently</u> and I <u>don't</u> feel <u>weaker</u> but <u>stronger</u> for seeking help.

I know I'm Me and You're <u>You</u>. But We're Us. And "Us" is not going to make it – Unless We <u>Both</u> get help to <u>change</u> and <u>grow</u>.

I've approached you before – About getting help – And you said – "I'll think about it" – But then <u>did nothing</u> about it.

Maybe you were hoping I'd forget – That time would pass and maybe things would get better between us by themselves.

Didn't happen did it. So it's time to get serious – <u>Really</u> serious. I know how you feel about being told – About being ordered to do something. Well, <u>this</u> is not an order I'm giving you – It's a <u>choice</u>. I'd like you to see it that way – But that will be up to you.

Either-Or – The <u>choice</u> comes down to this – <u>Either</u> you get <u>professional help</u> – <u>Or</u> I'm <u>leaving you</u> – (We're <u>done</u> – <u>Finished</u> – Fini.)

This is it! – Before you think there's someone else – There isn't – I still love you – But not as you are – Not how you <u>treat</u> me (<u>mistreat Me</u>) <u>mistreat Yourself</u>. If you don't get <u>help</u> to <u>change</u> and <u>get into</u> the <u>process of changing</u> – <u>I'm choosing not to live with you anymore</u>.

What is the <u>one</u> who <u>gave</u> the <u>ultimatum</u> looking for from the other?...

- The one – <u>who was given</u> – the ultimatum – And responded by getting help – Will want to include in their repertoire of behavioral changes – <u>Taking ownership</u> for their abusive behavior – Putting this taking responsibility – for the same – <u>into so many words to the other</u>.
- <u>Saying they're sorry</u> for having been so <u>mean</u> and <u>hurtful</u> with their <u>words</u> and <u>acts</u> – Then <u>promising</u> to <u>curtail</u>, <u>diminish</u>, and <u>ultimately extinguish such behavior</u>.

<u>Just words</u> – at this point – Sounding like they are sincerely meant – But again – keep in mind – behavioral changes involve not only <u>changing verbally</u> – But <u>non-verbally</u> as well – "By their <u>acts</u> one shall know them."

The <u>one</u> who <u>issues</u> the <u>ultimatum</u> is asking themselves – Is this enough to <u>forgive</u> them – And get past the situation – Needing more than this – from the other – would certainly be affected by how many times they may have heard variations of this before.

To make <u>true believers of them</u> they would have to see <u>consistency</u> over time – in <u>demonstrable behavioral change</u> – I.e. a <u>substantial reduction</u> – if not <u>extinction</u> – of <u>before perpetrated-abusive behavior</u> (If abusive behavior had had a <u>Physical</u> component there would be no "One More Time").

When is enough not enough? – <u>Extinction</u> or <u>near extinction</u> of <u>old behavior patterns</u> is not enough – Nor <u>should</u> be enough to <u>verify</u> that the <u>other</u> is <u>changing</u> – <u>New behaviors</u>, a <u>New Tone</u> to their <u>way of speaking</u> – That conveys <u>closeness</u> rather than <u>control</u> would need to be forthcoming – Essentially the <u>new behaviors</u> would be <u>replacing</u> the <u>old behaviors</u>.

[Having worked with many a client – who has finally become strong enough to give the other an ultimatum – I know that it hasn't always turned out the way I've been describing] – With some – Their other has balked and stalled – With some the other has said "No way" – I'm not going to get any help – I don't need any help – You're the one with the problem – You're the one who needs help. With some the other has said – "There's the door" – or – "I'm out of here."

If you're the <u>one</u> who is <u>giving</u> the other an ultimatum – You'll never know ahead of time how they'll react. The important thing is that <u>you</u> stay strong – In control of yourself. Hopefully you – (before this) – have gotten help for yourself – And that help continues – And regardless of the other's response – You will remain resolute and move forward.

If you're the <u>one getting</u> the ultimatum – I hope you will be able to listen to what your other is saying to you – Really saying to you – And that your <u>defenses</u> will not be so <u>high</u> – That nothing will get through. I hope you'll be able to see yourself for the moment – As the other is presenting you with how they see you – That your defenses don't find it necessary to completely <u>shield</u> you from the <u>reality</u> of what the other is perceiving and presenting – And be at least <u>reluctantly willing to seek help</u> – for your sake – as well as the sake of your other.

One gives the ultimatum – One sets a timetable for the other – It comes and goes – And nothing happens. The ball is now back in one's court. Of course it will be up to you! – No therapist should be instructing you what to do. – Assuming you have your own therapist working with you – They are there to support you – in whatever decision you make.

I'm sure your therapist will run by you the <u>realities they perceive</u> in your <u>situation</u> – And together with you weigh the <u>plusses</u> and <u>minuses</u> – The <u>costs</u> versus <u>rewards</u>. But whatever you decide – <u>They'll stick</u> with you to see you through <u>ramifications</u> of whatever <u>you choose</u> to do. [I guess I shouldn't be speaking for other therapists – but <u>I</u> sure as heck would.]

If one decides to leave – Or have the other leave – After the ultimatum has run its course to no avail – Then one will <u>continue</u> to <u>need therapeutic support</u> – To stay on track – And see this through.

If one thought they could do this – But now it's turning out they're <u>waffling</u> – They certainly need <u>therapeutic support all the more</u> – Because they are now in the <u>throes</u> of a <u>conflict</u> (<u>Avoidance-Avoidance</u>) – Probably, since either way has negatives. Such a conflict generates much <u>anxiety</u>. To get off of dead center one may resort to their Defenses – In particular the Defense of Rationalization.

<u>Rationalization as a defense</u> – Remember – In point of time – <u>One</u> has already perceived the other doing nothing about the ultimatum – And the ultimatum's time has expired!

The <u>Other</u> who was given the ultimatum <u>IS</u> the same Person <u>Before</u> and <u>After</u> the ultimatum. If the other in some way is <u>now looking better</u> to the one who gave the ultimatum – It's fair to suspect that the <u>Defense of Rationalization</u> is working hard to <u>reduce</u> the anxiety generated by the conflict – [I call this "Sweet Lemon Rationalization" – In that the other once perceived a "Lemon" is now perceived Somehow Sweeter.]

I wanted to write about Loyalty Because I said at the beginning – That I have been greatly troubled over the fact that Loyalty <u>both inside</u> and <u>outside</u> our Primary Relationship has been <u>remarkably missing</u>.

Perhaps one of the main reasons for this is our tendency to <u>narrowly define</u> our understanding of what Loyalty means <u>outside</u> our relationship – That we treat the other (and are treated by the other) fairly and with each other's best interests in mind – Unfortunately even this level of Loyalty is often not reached – When we are relating <u>outside</u> our primary relationship.

Moving <u>inside</u> our primary relationship I think we should be <u>looking for much more</u> out of loyalty than in our <u>outside</u> relationships – [This almost should go without saying.]

When we add Faithfulness to our expectations of Reciprocal Loyalty in our primary relationship – Plus we make a commitment to one another to Love, Cherish and be Loyal – to boot – Committing to all of this – I felt I needed to expand on what this meant to how we relate to each other – And treat each other in our Committed Primary Relationship.]

I decided to build a Construct of Loyalty which I felt would be part and parcel of what being Reciprocally Loyal to each other would look like – I.e. what being Loyal to each other would entail.

So I added Trustworthy, Responsible, Dependable, Accountable, Truthful to the mix and described what each of these Qualities of Loyalty would look like – When presented and practiced in our primary relationship.

Then I addressed what I thought Faithfulness – (Perceived as the most important quality of Loyalty) meant as far as the Commitment we made to each other in our Primary Relationship.

Specifically with regard to Faithfulness I wanted to make sure that Faithfulness would not be so narrowly defined that we would think of it as only applying if Either one of us, or Both of us had sexual relations with someone outside our Primary Relationship.

The caveat I issued to us all was – That we not therefore hasten to think that <u>only this Particular Breach of our Commitment</u> – to Faithfulness – Would <u>allow</u> us to <u>end</u> our committed relationship – If we so <u>chose</u> to do.

I felt – And continue to feel – That the tendency to look at our being Faithful to our other – Only in this narrowly defined way – Creates another tendency – <u>To not give enough attention to the other qualities of Love and Loyalty</u> that we Faithfully committed to.

When we committed to each other – We Pledged that we would be Faithful in Loving, Cherishing, and being Loyal to each other.

Essentially we were saying to each <u>other</u> – That they could believe in us – And we could believe in them – That we would be – And do – What we promised to.

What I wanted you – my reader – to do – And hope that you did – Was to perceive yourself and to perceive your other and <u>introspectively and</u>

extrospectively perceptually judge how you and your other come out – When taking the Litmus Test for Reciprocal Loving, Loyalty and Faithfulness.

I'm also hoping that after taking the Litmus Test you've been able to talk to each other about what each of you may need from the other – What you or your other may need to consider changing – Maybe one – or the other – or both of you – decide that you need some outside therapeutic support to help you change.

In any event, I wish for each of you – (For the sake of your primary relationship – And for your own psychological health and well-being – That you do the following – (Especially if you're not doing it already)…

Be Aware – Be Perceptive – Early On – Of things you don't like – (Along with things you do like, of course). Pay attention to how this social Personal Exchange – you have with your other – is panning out – I.e. costs versus rewards.

Assert early on what you need – Don't be Brushed Aside – Avoided – or Ignored – Have respect for yourself. Respect should be <u>reciprocal</u>, as <u>loving, caring, nurturing, supporting, trusting</u>.

If not – Why not! – What's going on that you're <u>not getting</u> these from the other – Nor do you feel like – (And therefore you may not be) – <u>Giving</u> them to the other.

Your relationship is not something to be <u>lightly regarded</u> – Nor <u>taken for granted</u> – It is to be given a very <u>high priority</u> in the scheme of things.

Take <u>good care</u> of yourselves and your relationship – Do not count on it <u>to take care</u> of itself.

And for goodness sakes – Don't you let it get to the point where it <u>becomes necessary</u> to <u>give</u> or <u>receive</u> an ultimatum – <u>Better late</u> than <u>never</u> – Maybe – But I wouldn't <u>take a chance</u> on that – If you <u>can help it</u>.

Blessings
Take Good Care,
Doc Ken
K. L. Fischer, PhD

About the Author

- Dr. Kenneth L. Fischer (affectionately called Doc Ken) has been in helping professions his entire adult life.

- Founder and pastor of Peace Lutheran Church, Disco, MI

- Pastor of Mt. Olive Lutheran Church, Grand Rapids, MI

- Junior High School teacher 8th grade English, 9th grade Latin, Muskego, MI

- First psychologist in the history of the Men's Unit, State Prison, Lowell, FL

- Dr. Fischer received his PhD in Personality Psychology, Michigan State University, East Lansing, MI

- His doctoral work was in Person Perception

- An instructor and lecturer, Dept. of Psychology, University of Wisconsin, Milwaukee, WI

- Also taught at various colleges throughout the Milwaukee-Metro area, namely Milwaukee Area Technical College, Mt. Mary College, Alverno College, and at Carthage College, Racine, WI

- Dr. Fischer has been a practicing psychologist in his own clinic for the past thirty-five years, treating adult couples and individuals

- His areas of expertise are in Personality and Person Perception

- His specialty is Personality Disorders

- Support Therapy Clinic is located in Hartland, WI

Other Books by Kenneth L. Fischer, PhD

Closeness Without Control:
The Key To A Loving Reciprocal Relationship Of
Assertive Independent Equals

Seeing Ourselves As We See Others See Us:
Our Personality Develops Through Person Perception
and Self-Experience

The Gray Area Of Psychological Abuse:
Abusee? Abuser? Or Both? How Can We Tell?
What Can We Do?

**Psychologically Speaking What Are We Really
Saying?**
The Music Behind The Music Behind Our Words

Don't Like The Way It Is - Change It:
Changing Before Or After An Ultimatum

We've Got Personality!
Now What?

Don't Be A Stranger (To Yourself):
Go Outside Yourself To Get Inside Yourself Then Turn
Yourself Inside Out

**The Art And Efficacy Of Managing Person
Perceptions:**
Manipulation In Its Highest Psychotherapeutic Sense

In Defense Of Defensiveness:
Knowing Our Defenses, Lowering Our Defenses,
Living With Our Defenses

The Incomparable Spunkerface and Company:
Heaven Sent - Heaven Bent

www.ingramcontent.com/pod-product-compliance
Lightning Source LLC
Chambersburg PA
CBHW070811280726

48660CB00015B/326